The Literary Connection

Volume II

My Canada!

Editors:

Cheryl Antao-Xavier

Nina Munteanu

Merridy Cox Bradley

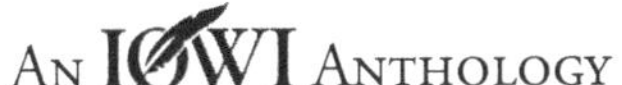

THE LITERARY CONNECTION
VOLUME II

Publisher: In Our Words Inc.
www.inourwords.ca
inourwords@bell.net

Book design: Shirley Aguinaldo

Cover Art: John Di Leonardo
The triptych "Book of Hours: Canada Is"

Library and Archives Canada Cataloguing in Publication
The literary connection / editors: Cheryl Antao-Xavier, Nina Munteanu, Merridy Cox Bradley.

"An IOWI anthology"
Contents: v. 2. My Canada! / editors: Cheryl Antao-Xavier, Nina Munteanu, Merridy Cox-Bradley.

ISBN 978-1-926926-58-2 (v. 2 : paperback)

1. Canadian literature (English)--21st century. I. Antao-Xavier, Cheryl, editor II. Munteanu, Nina, editor III. Cox Bradley, Merridy, editor

PS8251.1.L58 2014 C810.8'006 C2014-905856-X

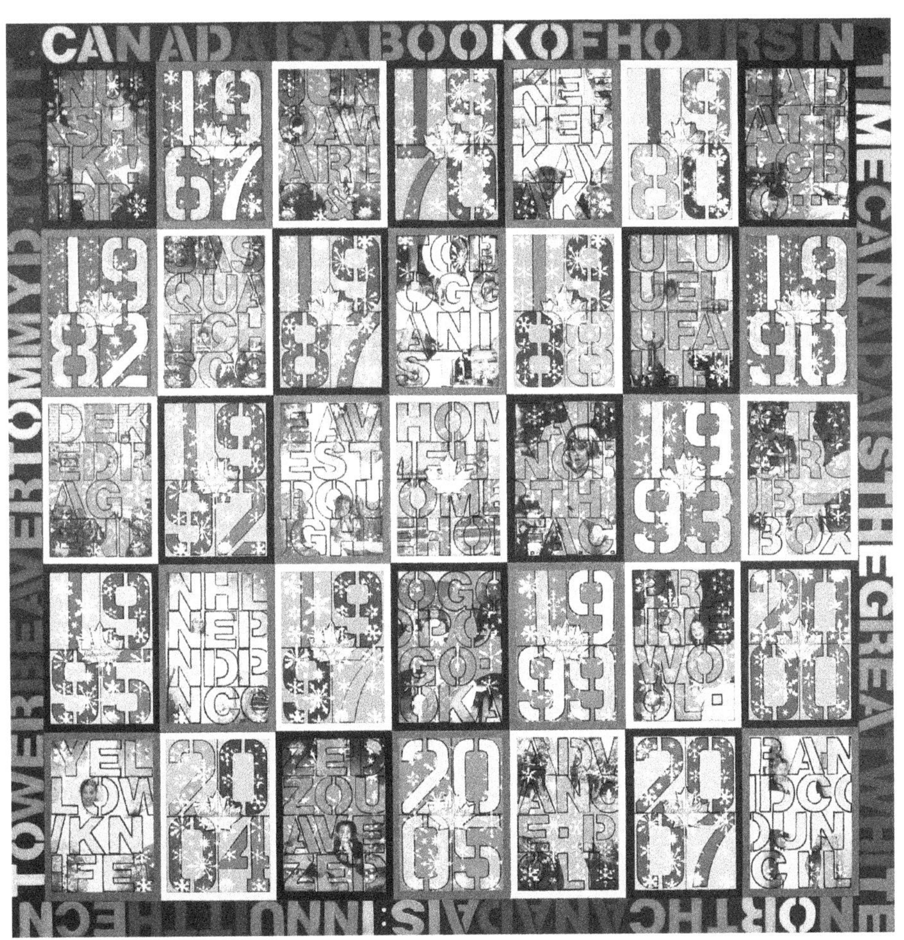

The triptych "Book of Hours: Canada Is" - Oil/Mixed Media on Canvas, 4' X 12', 1995 - 1997. (©John Di Leonardo)

"I see the paintings in the Book of Hours series as objects of spiritual meditation for a secular age."

John Di Leonardo is an artist and poet from Brooklin, Ontario, Canada. John is represented by Art Dialogue Gallery in Toronto.

AUTHORS

IMAGES
(in order of appearance)

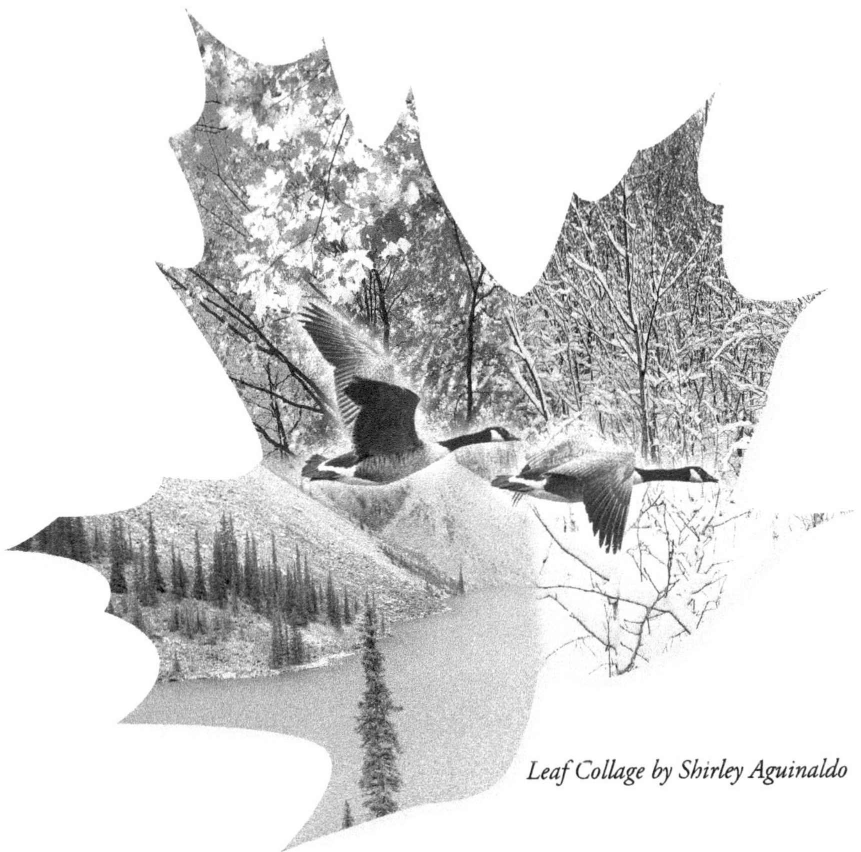

Leaf Collage by Shirley Aguinaldo

WELCOME TO THE ANTHOLOGY:

The Literary Connection

VOLUME II

This year's anthology call prompted an enthusiastic response to the theme of *My Canada!* Twenty-six Canadian authors write of their connection to the land they call home. Canada's natural beauty forms the backdrop of poems and stories of life 'then' and 'now;' of coping with the elements; of nostalgia for a simpler time, the old country; and quiet pride in the 'spirit' of a nation that has welcomed settlers and held on to its core altruistic values.

"Isn't it wonderful to think how this same sky was seen by my great-grandfather?... I'm the luckiest man in the world [for being here]."

"Awakening to the sound of the loon on the lake, / I grab my blanket, step outside and watch the morning break."

"the pale blue sky draws a tidy line / across the lake's grey eyelid / a seagull planes down / onto the wet pebbles / struts by a stone inukshuk"

"Unconditional love I seek to give and receive / With love and acceptance I can live free to be me"

"The horror deep-embedded / lasted long after armistice / heavy tears continue to fall / in many a beer mug or wineglass / continues to saturate many a pillow"

"scents of oregano and basil emanate from the pot / stimulating nostalgia / wooden spoon stained with years / of family tradition and folklore / stirring secrets and untold legends"

"My Hebrew is a pretense / I have created myself / wrapped in a Canadian shawl"

"I bring richness from the East / And add it to the wealth of my home and 'native' land"

"I write / To excavate my past / And to chisel a peephole / into Canadian living. / Trying to understand."

"I do miss the old country, but Canada is my new home now."

"'Canadian' is in the land, and in the history, it's in the people, and part of our society / Canada – so hard to describe, is simply alive."

We thank all the contributors to this anthology for sharing their creative talent and stories and making this an awesome collection.

The Editors

Kate Marshall Flaherty

SKINWALKER

after Norval Morriseau's painting of a shape-shifter

Forgive me,
I do not know your story,
nor have I walked a single footfall in your shoes
on the long red road;
I don't have words for "sorry" in Ojibway.
In sign language, it is the rub
of soft fist on chest,
gentle friction over the heart,
like this.

Sorry,
I only know your name's five syllables;
they are famous now,
a mark on the map.
What I do know,
leaning on a cold wall
in a Buckhorn gallery,
is the deeper-than-lichen teal,
rich beaver-pelt brown,
perfect-August-sky blue,
and the slick black
of algae fingers in a river—
I know these colours
in the shapes
you have left for me.

Your painting has gotten under my skin.

I come back to it
after sighting barns
in the gallery
with winter night-lights bright as hay,

sunsets like copper pots,
birch blobs thick as fish soup
with silver scales.

I return to your Skinwalker
on reverent soles.
This painting grounds me—
its clear lines and circles,
yellow-red eye dots,
its colours solid, clear.

I hide under its hide a while,
camp out in awe.

Let us rest here, shape shifter,
pitch our tent together,
my supernatural brother.

Wrapped in animal fur,
what is that split sphere
like a ladybug in your sight?
that stinging point
at your foot?

See, I address now the art's flat face,
not the artist.
Norval, ghost-walker,
you have changed yourself
into man-beast-bird-frame.

You have changed me,
for I want to see more
of these three bright eyes.

I come full circle:
Migwetch,[1]
the only word I know.

---

[1] *Migwetch* is thanks in Ojibway

MAGNETAWAN

Half and half—
this astounding split seems odd
from my perch on the pine island.

One side of the sky
blue and mid-day bright,
the other a tumble of dark and mutinous clouds

gathering yin and yang momentum—
the bright side with one seed of wispy black,
the ominous side purpling with a point of sun.

Heavy weather pushes in, pudding-thick.
And settles in my belly.

I love the gathering roll of plum clouds, the electric air;
the rise of wind hackling the hairs on my neck.

The excited birds cling to branches too.
Peeper frogs float still as lily pads.
The loons go under and stay.

The wind whips up, clouds slide in.
Waves of finger-paint darken the page.

Weather's bruise pressed
on my sternum
leaving a soft depression
streaked with rain.

MUKWA

I am mother
Mukwa
she-bear
bearing my quiver-lip teeth
I splinter the trees
if you get between me
and my cubs

Beware
my thunder
that pops jack pine cones
right off their scraggly branches
when I claw the air
land ripples
on the dusty earth

My licks
slide sweet as honey
over my cubs' ears
and I am soft-pawed
scooping of silvery fish

Odayin, love,
swarms our summers like bees

Yet I can surprise you with my charge
of raw meat-muscle
she-bear tendon—instinct
and grizzle
if you threaten
to harm my cubs

I am awoken hibernator,
queen of the mountain,
grizzly tree-climber
and I can smash you,

send you to earth
like a felled log—

heed my
swarm warning!

Even my mate-man
can't rip the bark off rage
the way I can—

When I am
barred from my young,
I am
Misabe, Grizzly
she-bear
roaring a warning
that trembles the mountains
sending scree
down the slope

LOST

Once I learned the word
migwetch
in a place of sweet grass and sunlight

I felt many earth-words—
the drumming pound,
Manitoulin sand packed
beneath our feet
a circle of fancy dance
and jingle jumps rejoicing
recalling how women were the first drummers
plucking beats
out of needle and hoop quill, skin

I had a drum teacher once long ago,
we all did
in the womb
fire earth wind singing like water
timbrel and tongue
cedar boughs on poles
to shade our tender white skin—

gifts we were given
of cloth and craft
the book of strawberry stories
and a ladybug
medicine wheel

the hush of a dropped eagle feather

DIG

Children's Site at the ROM, Toronto

Locky's hair. Still blonde as beach,
drips into the huge box,
goggles arc his brow

He is lost—
In the grit-sand-shovel-brush-away-inspection
of it all; blowing dry earth
from bone, exposing ribbed ridges,
sweeping grit from grooves in vertebrae.

He goes deep
                concentrates with every cell,

crawls over the lip of the sandbox
and into ancient sight,
gets right into the fossils
and back to bedrock.

He doesn't read yet
the "keep out" sign,
lost as he is
in history's hairline fissures,
Hieroglyphs
and mysterious mounds.

Deep in dirt
and the now

absorbed in desert dust

he becomes
the dig

BOVINE POEM

your liquid eyes that reflect the sky

your soft pink nose
still glistening from the lick
of your thick cow tongue

your ear-tag
nose ring
branded hide

all prove to me your tenderness

cowhands sear your flesh
and pierce it
while still you chew your cud—
an edible reflection on patience—
as you mull over sweet grass
(your velvet forehead furrowed)
swishing your tassel-tail
and nosing clover

what makes you kneel before a rain
share your manger with babes
let your milk
be milked for others' offspring?

your crooning stable lowing
soothes the stall

your moo rumbles
up from the earth

RE-ENTRY

Red-eyed jet lag
and a parched throat

it feels as if I've been crying
all night
or drinking gin

but I blink and blink
as I've done neither
yet
flying home from Banff
Air Canada

On a dull silver wing
I watch the sun
rise maraschino

I notice the tiny lines
and rivets on the metal
slide of a droplet
down the porthole
looking out over a sea of peachy clouds

the yellow rheum of city sighs
visible as we descend
ears popping

I don't care
for Sprite or peanuts
the crinkle of snack wrappers
and passenger banter over the engine boom jarring
after months of Cascade Mountain breeze
and Rundle Summit silence

somewhere beyond
this is your captain speaking

I buckle up and brace myself for re-entry
as we slide into a summer haze
of smog warnings and cement

the CN tower points its slick needle
the tip a sharp contrast to rounded mountains
I wince and readjust my vision
and think of the Bow River
valley of your body
I left behind

(All poems by Kate Marshall Flaherty are from Stone Soup, *published by Quattro Books, 2014)*

Kate Marshall Flaherty *published her most recent book,* Stone Soup *with Quattro Books, the same year as* Reaching V, *with Guernica Editions. She has been published in Canadian journals such as CV2, Descant, Grain, Malahat Review and Vallum, and in international anthologies such as* Not A Muse, *and American journals such as* Saranac Review. *She was Shortlisted for Descant's Best Canadian Poem, the Pablo Neruda Poetry Prize, the Robert Frost Poetry Prize and Thomas Merton Poetry of the Sacred Award. She guides Golden Rule Leadership Retreats, Writing as a Spiritual Practice Workshops and yoga classes. She is now the Toronto Representative for the League of Canadian Poets.*

Peta-Gaye Nash

A *LIKKLE* HALLOWEEN OBSESSION

The season was changing, altogether too fast, and the hot, dry summer had given way to a balmy fall. Outside, the bright sunlight shone on the golds, oranges, and red that surrounded Jean's house in a dazzling display of autumn brilliance.

Jean turned away from the window, trying hard to concentrate on her task of sorting through the Halloween decorations that filled every bit of floor space in the room. She wailed the cry of a woman who had reached breaking point. She rocked back and forth, clutching at her dark brown hair, freshly-dyed to hide the grey that made her look like an old woman. She laughed as this thought crossed her mind. She *was* an old woman. No matter how people said sixty is the new fifty, she looked sixty. Yet, she felt twenty inside: young, vulnerable, and helpless without John.

Every time she went up to his room to give him breakfast, lunch or a small snack, he whispered 'Halloween' through parched lips. At first, she pretended to ignore him, but the last time, he'd clutched her hands in desperation, made her look at him and he croaked insistently, 'Halloween.' She'd looked at him in horror. How could he expect this of her? He was selfish. She already had to cook for him, clean up after him and there was no money coming in because she'd taken time off work. It was silly and unrealistic of him to expect any more of her.

She cried as she looked around the room at the life-sized skeletons waiting to come to life at the push of a remote button. John had named each and given them all gruesome stories of death. There was a witch stirring a pot of witch's brew, a child missing half a brain, rats, bats, large hairy spiders, and tombstones with funny lines:

Here lies Clyde whose life was full
Until he tried to milk a bull.

Here lies my wife
I bid her goodbye
She rests in peace
Now so do I.

Every single year John took out the tombstones, he laughed as if reading them for the first time. At first she was scornful, but over time, she learned to laugh with him and they made up stories about Clyde, that he must have been the village idiot. Whenever anyone did something that was silly like bad driving and cutting people off in traffic, they said, that person is a Clyde. They'd nod in agreement and laugh. John made life funny. John made life bearable.

Jean looked around at the wires and started another bout of bawling. Tears ran down her face and she lay on the floor and pounded her fists into it as if beating the floor was going to make any difference.

Some of the garage had already been set up with decorations. John had set the stage, but there was still too much to be done and Halloween was a week away. Usually by this time, John would've been halfway through it all.

When they'd come to Canada, they were in their thirties with two young children. They were church-going people and the other Jamaican immigrants at the church looked down on Halloween, said it had roots in the occult and the Bible was clear on this. October 31st was the Festival of the Dead. At first, John and Jean wouldn't allow their girls to go trick or treating. They turned off their lights and didn't give out candy, but John had a natural curiosity about all things. It was what Jean loved about him. He was an extrovert and liked nothing better than talking to people and roaming the neighbourhood being social. One Halloween night as they were coming home from Church, they saw what seemed to be the entire neighbourhood gathered around the house of a man whose entire house was decorated. Neighbours were laughing and chatting.

"I'm going to do that next year," said John his face animated. "I hear what the church says but it's just a night to dress up and get candy. I'm going to outdo that man's house. I'm going to make sure the neighbourhood gathers at my house. I'm going to offer small glasses of red wine—I'll tell people it's blood. I'll be dressed as a vampire. You're going to be dressed as a witch. Do you know they do trick or drink in the small towns in Saskatchewan for the adults? What a wonderful tradition."

"I'm not going as a witch. I'm not going as anything. Who have you been talking to? You come to a new country and you're suddenly going to be a different person and change all your values. And you're giving people alcohol?" Jean kissed her teeth, frowned and crossed her arms.

"It's just for fun. We have to fit in, Jean. This is all a part of coming to a new country." You can't just come here and act like you're in your own country. You have to embrace what is here."

"But Canada accepts everybody. You don't have to celebrate this tradition."

"Canada accepts everybody but it doesn't mean they like everybody. Jean, we live here now. I want to be a part of it, not living on the outside looking in."

After Halloween, John shopped all the party stores for the discounts. He stored moving skeletons and rubber masks, bloodied dismembered limbs in the guest room for the following year. He spent five hundred dollars on Halloween decorations that first year. Jean didn't talk to him for a week.

By the time Halloween came, she had forgotten John's plans. Two weeks before October 31st, she came home to find John stringing pumpkin lights along the garage door.

"I said I was sick at work so I could come home and get started," he said, barely looking at her and stretching precariously on the ladder to hang the pumpkins.

"Just mind you don't fall and kill yourself doing that foolishness," she said going inside, muttering under her breath that she wasn't going to help.

"You remind me of Chevy Chase in that Christmas movie," she yelled out the window after two hours of John sticking tombstones in the front garden to create a gravesite. "You're obsessed."

"This house is going to be the best house in the neighbourhood. All the neighbours are going to come. You see, Jean, when in Rome, do as the Romans. It's about embracing the culture," he said testing the witch who was turning a stick in a brew. "Listen to this witch laugh," he said standing back to view his creation.

More changes were to follow. They changed churches from the evangelical church in the Jamaican community to a quieter Anglican church in their newer more affluent neighbourhood.

"Don't you miss our own people?" Jean asked one morning.

"Sometimes, but people are people. You know what I love about this country, Jean? I have friends from all over the globe. I know how to say 'how are you' in seven languages."

"But it's not the same. There's not the same understanding as there is with people from your own culture," Jean argued.

"We're all the same. Everybody want a likkle money, everybody want to be safe and healthy, everybody want dem pickney to have an education. Jean, we no different from anybody else in dis country."

Year after year, John's Halloween decorations got bigger and more elaborate. He dressed as Count Dracula every year and offered tiny shot glasses of wine to the adults. He put on a spectacle for the children. A projector showed images of bats flying on the walls of the house, the graveyard in the front had fifteen headstones, the life-sized skeletons he called Marge and Louis sat on a bench waiting for the children. Jean gave out the candy while John socialized with the neighbours. In time, he knew their names and the names of their children. He stopped to pet their dogs. Jean didn't know how he had the energy to socialize and to set up a show for the children every Halloween.

Jean didn't know where the time went. Their children grew up and left home and still, John decorated for the children of the neighbourhood. He said it was for the children, but Jean knew he loved it, getting dressed up, awing everyone with his creativity, hearing his name all night, "Hey John," swapping stories, laughing and giving out candy. It burned her out, but he was always sorry when it was over. "We did good again this year," he'd say. "You see how people loved it, not just the children but the adults too. You see how scared the little ones were? Marge and Louis love it. It's the one night of the year they get any attention," he said referring to his skeletal couple. John was a big kid.

Now he was stuck upstairs riddled with cancer, too weak to get out of bed and put up decorations. He wanted her to do it. She who had never done it before. It was the hardest thing he'd ever asked of her. Just two months ago, he'd gotten his diagnosis. He didn't have a lot of time left so Jean didn't understand why he was still obsessed with Halloween. Jean dried her tears and went upstairs.

"John, I can't do it. It's too much. I don't know where to start."

"Can't disappoint the kids. Everyone expects it. Start with tombstones. Easiest. Make the gravesite." It took five minutes to get all these instructions out. He was tired. She caressed his cheek. "Okay," she said.

The tombstones were easy. They had little stakes at the bottom that she stuck into the grass. There was a large skeleton that belonged with the set, half buried. Jean took it out of its box and lay him in the garden with the tombstones.

"The tombstones are done, all fifteen of them. What's next?" She held John's hand. His skin was grey.

"The witch stirring the brew. Easy. She plugs in."

Jean couldn't believe she finished the night before Halloween. Luckily too because it fell on a Wednesday and she'd gone back to work that day. A Jamaican nurse came to look after John and she viewed the decorations with a mien of disgust and admiration at the same time.

Jean dressed herself carefully. She applied green face paint and drew in black lines where her natural wrinkles fell. She put on a long green nose that hooked around her head and put on her pointed witch hat. John had bought the costume five years ago for her and she usually grumbled when she put it on. Now she felt sadness. It would take a miracle for John to get past this. They both knew in their bones it was his last Halloween. The doctor had told him to put his affairs in order and the will they'd made twenty years ago when the children were young had been updated.

It was a beautiful night, fifteen degrees and not a cloud in the sky. Last year it rained yet John still stood in the rain with his costume, soaked and cold, and got pneumonia.

"Never again," Jean told him. "If it rains, you're not going outside."

Jean stepped out into the warm autumn night. The garden which was ablaze in the day was now shrouded in mystery and ghoul. Ghosts hung from the trees twirled in the wind. She turned on the witch and watched her slowly turning the brew. She flicked a switch for the hanging pumpkins and the projector for the flying bats. She watched them swirl on the wall, mesmerized by the shadows. Everything was in place. She waited for the children to come and stare, so in awe were they that sometimes John had to remind them to go get candy.

Jean was nervous. She was not sociable and shied away from small talk with the neighbours. They started to come, one by one, small kids at first and then the bigger ones. Everyone asked for John. He told her not to tell anyone he was dying, only sick at the moment and unable to take part this year.

But nosy Martin from the Ukraine pressed her saying with his guttural accent, "I can't believe John is not here. Where's the red wine? I don't believe it. It's not Halloween without John," until she finally blurted out, "He has cancer okay? He's too sick to come down." Martin's mouth opened and closed like a fish. "Let me see him. I can't believe it."

"But he doesn't want to see anybody. He doesn't want anybody to see him like this."

Before Jean knew what happened, Martin and Mohammed from Egypt had gone up and lifted John downstairs and onto the driveway where they made him comfortable beside Marge and Louis.

"This is a fitting place for me, isn't it?" smiled John ruefully and Martin laughed and hugged him. Tears rolled down Jean's eyes and smeared her makeup, the green and black mixing into a muddy colour, as she watched everyone hug John, the adults and the children alike.

People she hardly spoke to squeezed her hand and told her to call on them anytime. Caitlin the caterer, a woman who Jean always felt was too cozy with John, handed her a business card. "I'm going to do dinner for you this week," she said. "Call me if John needs special food or if you have allergies." Martin said he'd take down the decorations the next day for her. "And I'll help you put them up next year," he added. "If you want to, of course."

Jean nodded. She couldn't imagine a life without John.

He was tired and couldn't smile anymore. Jean asked Martin and Mo to carry him up to bed. The crowd thinned and petered out. Jean joked that she wouldn't forget the wine next year.

"We'll be sure to remind you," someone laughed.

Jean stood in the doorway before she closed the door and watched a golden leaf fall from a maple tree and flutter to the ground. She breathed in the scent of fall, moist leaves and wood, the freshness of pine and evergreen, and on this night, the sweetness of candy.

The cool fall air entered her nostrils and she closed her eyes and whispered, "We did good again this year, John."

EXCERPT FROM SHORT STORY
I TOO HEAR THE DRUMS

1986, Toronto, Canada

I am excited to be in Canada, 'foreign,' as we call any white country. Excited about new beginnings. If you stay too long on an island, it gets stale.

My parents drop me off at York University. I chose York only because a guy I liked was going there. A friend of mine chose York because it has the highest population of blacks, the Canadian version of D.C.'s Howard.

This is where I taste my first bit of anger. Someone calls me a black b— because we have a disagreement at the fast food restaurant where I am working to earn a little extra money. I decide I have to be black. I seem to have little in common with white Canadian girls who go beer drinking as a hobby and head to the ski slopes for March break. I have to try too hard with them. I head to the Caribbean Student Association where I am told that I cannot join. It's a club for West Indians, I am told.

"But I am Jamaican. I was born in Jamaica. I am West Indian."

The guy I'm speaking to is Dwayne. I know this because someone in a red, green and black t-shirt walks by and greets him with the fist to fist, 'respect.' Dwayne, tall, muscular and black, also donning a t-shirt with a Bob Marley face spread, has that typical Torontonian-Jamaican accent. I can tell it's been cultivated. Has this jackass ever even been to Jamaica? He tells me I don't sound Jamaican. I've heard this many times before but usually it's said with interest, surprise. People assume I've been living in England. No, people, I want to shout, I went to London once for two weeks, hardly enough time to acquire a British accent. But this coming from Dwayne, is accusatory, angry.

"I'm from Jamaica," I insist again.

"Prove it," he says. "Can you hear the drums?"

I am taken aback. I feel slapped in the face.

"Were you born in Jamaica?" I ask.

"No, but I can hear the drums."

"I can hear the drums," I say, "but I don't need to wear my culture on my t-shirt. It's in my blood. Screw your association."

When I walk away, I think, what drums? He wasn't in Jamaica for the brain drain, the political riots, the empty supermarket shelves, the senseless murders where we all knew people who died. He was in rich North America learning how to be Jamaican second-hand.

I spend four years at university never once attending the Caribbean Students Association. I feel strangely disconnected from any race. White guys treat me like an exotic fruit, some are brave enough to taste, but mostly they wrinkle their noses. Black guys like me eventually, when they discover I really am Jamaican. Their line is always, "You don't look Jamaican." When I hear this, I too put them in a special category. Ignorant. They say this same line to my Jamaican friends who look Chinese or Indian or white.

These are the people who don't know Jamaica at all, don't know its rich history, know nothing about the many immigrants who set foot on its sandy shores, don't know our motto is 'out of many, one people.' Yeah, ignoramus, screw your association.

1995 Toronto, Canada

I get a job. I finally get a decent job that doesn't include serving drunken pre-adults or lecherous old men. I am teaching English as a second language at a small private college outside of Toronto. I spend my days teaching not only language but Canadian culture.

It all goes smoothly until I take the students on a field trip to Toronto and they see a white girl lip-locked in a passionate embrace with a black boy. They are around seventeen, maybe more. Who knows these days. Then the students see an Asian girl holding hands with a black guy. They gasp at these couples and tell me it's not right. Black should be with black. All races should stick to their own. I take a deep breath and try to explain apartheid. I try to convey that their views are wrong, out-dated, and totally alien in this new land to which they have come.

My students are all from India and no matter what I say, I cannot change their views. I think, 'Oh no, my children will go to school with their children.' Why come here then? Why use Canada as a hotel for its freedoms while keeping yourself in a prison?'

At first, I tell myself it's just their upbringing but I get mad when they tell me they don't like black skin colour, they don't like black hair and they bring their fingers up to their head and make a disgusted face. They don't see me as black because I look like them. When our arms touch, my skin is no different from theirs. It's my hair that is different and even then, they don't see it as 'black' hair. I notice this. I don't look black so people feel they can say anything. I am mad, mad when they see a blonde-haired girl and they tell me she is beautiful when I see that she is just a plain Jane.

I get mad that they don't see that the blood of Africa runs through their veins, that their DNA contains the genes of those first people who set foot out of that continent. I get mad that they've brought their 'us' and 'them' mentality, and don't see that one big bang explosion created us all.

This anger makes me weary and I wonder how those great men of history kept fighting for justice through all the dissension.

2002, Toronto, Canada

I get married to a mixed-race man and we produce two more mixed-race people for the world. A boy who is darker than the girl, his hair is thick and curly. His skin colour is like honey, golden reddish-brown. The girl could be white, creamy, except for the giveaway hair, wildly curly from roots to ends, a fuzzy pale halo around her head. To me, they are mesmerizingly beautiful. People will ask them, what is your background, where are you from, what are your parents, is one white and one black, what are you really? They will have to explain the whole thing.

Or, maybe not. Maybe they'll grow up in a Canada where cultural differences are no big deal, and where nobody really gives a damn if they hear the drums of a place they've never called 'home.'

(From I too Hear the Drums*—short stories, revised edition, IOWI, 2015)*

Peta-Gaye Nash *was born in Kingston, Jamaica, but has made Canada home for twenty years.* I Too Hear the Drums *is her first short story collection published in 2010. Her work has appeared in several anthologies and she has written six children's books. Peta-Gaye won the 2015 Marty Awards for Emerging Literary Arts and in 2013 she received an honorable mention for the same award. A graduate of McMaster University, Peta-Gaye teaches English as a Second Language in Mississauga, Ontario, where she lives with her husband and four children.*

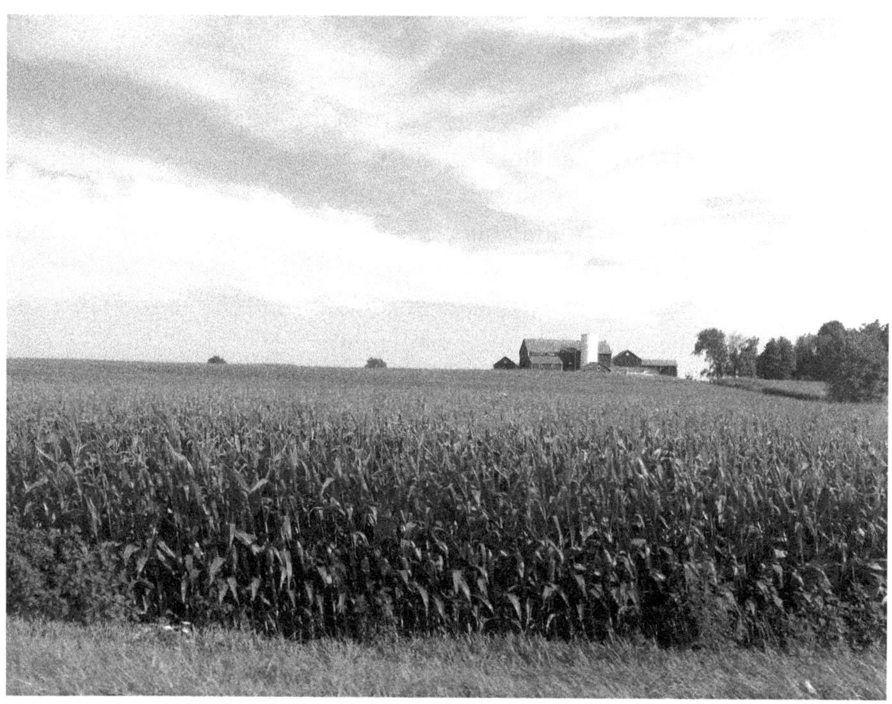

Family Farmhouse in Southwest Ontario by John B. Lee

John B. Lee

SUNSET OUTSIDE OF SHANNON ON OUR LAST NIGHT IN IRELAND

In the summer of 1994, three generations of my family and I returned to Ireland, the land of my ancestors. On the last evening of our visit to the old country, my father and I sat on the lawn looking west to sunfall shadowed on the green fields outside of city Shannon. The laundered B&B bedding flapped on the line in the foreground like sheets full of wind from ships of passage. It was a lovely evening, quiet with the cool warm breath of the world.

My thoughts were of the bittersweet sort we feel when things are so nearly perfect they almost wound us with their beauty. This was the end of our sojourn. Tomorrow we would fly home. My parents would remember this trip as the best of their lives. My mother still lingers over the photographs of us all on the Island that our forebears had left the century before. I sat in the sad and looked to my father who watched the dusk fall in the far and wondered what he thought.

"What are you thinking about, Dad?" I asked him, hoping he'd say that to him this failing light was a common covenant and this country we'd seen was the best.

"I'm thinking of home, son," he said and he sighed. "I'm thinking, no matter how lovely this place, it doesn't hold a candle to Canada. I'm thinking of the farm where I live and how much more beautiful it is even than this."

And so it has always been for him. I'd heard him say the same before and I've heard him say the same a dozen times since then. I've overheard those very words spoken to a stranger he'd met as he sat on a bench near the Spanish market in Los Angeles. I've heard his conviction on the steps of Capitol Hill in Washington and I've heard it overlooking the great Pacific Ocean from the tar-sand beaches of Carpinteria, California, with the coastal mountain Christmas majesty looming behind us. He loves the land he was born to most and best.

Two years ago when he and I and mother sat on the home veranda at the farm, looking out at the blue heavens where a double rainbow bent horizon to horizon before us, my father said, "Isn't it wonderful to think how this same sky was seen by my great-grandfather before the land was cleared? I'm the luckiest man in the world," he'd said, meaning "here" meaning "being here now" meaning "being home, born at home, living at home, and growing old with the prospect of being here forever, connected to this life by knowing this place, knowing his place in the world, fixed exactly here on this very farm." To him, this house, these barns, these familiar acres were indeed better than all other places.

Others might ask, "But how do you know, George? You've never lived anywhere else." Others might wonder, but not he. These one-hundred-and-fifty fecund acres of land in the heart of southwestern Ontario bring him as close to the Garden as any man might come. His house, the only house he's ever known, is a perfect homely paradise. This year, he's off to cruise the Amazon. He's reading about Brazil. I'm sure he'll tell the captain where he lives and why. He'll cross the burning line with pictures in his wallet he'll gladly show to strangers in the sub-equatorial heat, while winter freezes the water at the barn and my uncle shovels his way to the truck from the door.

"I wish I were home," he will say, "I wish I were home."

(From The Farm on the Hill He Calls Home, *Black Moss Press, 2004)*

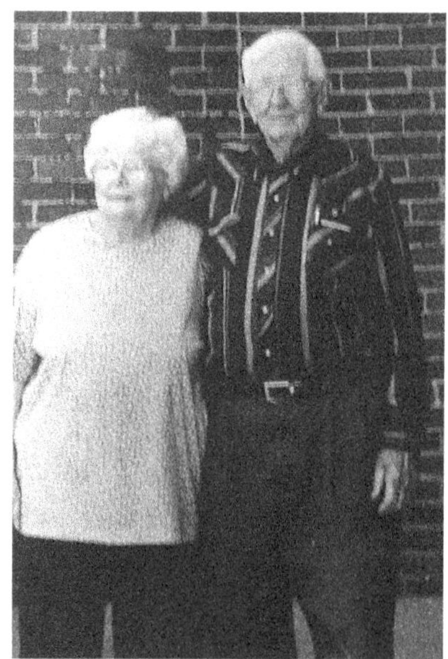

John B. Lee's parents, George and Lillian Lee. Photo taken by Bob Hill.

I TOO CAN SHOW THE WAY

Written in the Canadian Arctic

Where would you lead me friend?
into what future
and from what past
and by what light guide
and for what purpose go
and to what end
and with what faith …
for if I follow
where the hills are hard
and if I cross cruel rivers
on the way
stepping stone by stone
between the foams and froths
that break the water's voice
and if I look to see
who comes behind
by my example then
we share a path
and breathe to climb
and step against the slope
to see the valley's hard green ease
beyond a blind horizon's call
and if you'd named the dangers
one by one
and sent those glories free before
how then
to temper knowing
if I do not touch the stones the rivers touch
how then to look upon the map
and say
see there, we went together
    I too can show
the way.

(From The Echo of Your Words Has Reached Me, *Mekler and Deahl, 1998)*

SEND ME THE NAMES

she lived at the last
in Durban by the sea
she dwelt in rooms of privilege
thick in swarms of change
and though she thought herself in paradise
she also saw the suffering
and ruined earth
the awful denouement of nations
shaped by map's ephemeral surmise
black orchids and the dragon's jaw
the golden morning
and the crimson hiss of night
her future now
in volumes of the past
with old Hiroshima blooming and reborn
as something
rising from the rubble
still in flame
and lines demarking cities
of the mind
too high to climb

Apartheid where she lives
and war in Seoul about to start
she sent
a postcard to the farm
addressing issues
like a songbird chirming
on the cusp of coming storm

tell me of the boys from home
send me the names
among the Execroi—
the volunteers—

she said she longed to climb the fence
to fetch the milk—
or drift like weather
on a carpet bound for Canada
again—

and as she wrote
those lines

the globe in shadow
changed its mask of shades

and nations faded in and out
as though from blackened whites
of cloud-crossed snow

and though true ink
might grip a moment
as it dries

it also blots its counter page
with unintended lies

(From Into a Land of Strangers, *work in progress)*

THERE IS A NATION

There is a nation in my mind
not the land
nor salmon maps
nor memory, nor names
nor a gathering of huts
nor tracks a scar
across the flats shaking the wheat
and blasting the snow
from its share of the hills

nor ragged green pines
whistling lonely
under the dream-wet brush
of a wolf's moon-dipped tail
nor all the invented borders
no, there is
in my mind
a nation of long silence
spinning down light
as a lover's touch
telling me life begins
with all the beauty and blasphemy
of living exactly here
in the wordless landscape
of home

(From Tongues of the Children, *Black Moss Press, 1996)*

THE BEAUTY OF DYING

yesterday, we went driving
where the wind was waltzing the wheat
  and the tall timothy
  was just such soft green
  it seemed dusted by the light
  in the exaggerated lamp shadow
of the hour of the day
  and you told me
  how you loved this Essex county
  lake-bottom land
where the trees in the distance
  waved a long farewell
shrunk as they were in the latitude and longitude
of a far-away Souwesto sorrow
  as if seeing us gone
had brought them out weeping
  in windrows
weeping and dousing for rivers
  and we stopped
where a Catholic doorway
  faced fathoms with its frontale
  yielding to flow
and dreaming Brûlé, dreaming de la Roche
dreaming Brébeuf
  and his black robed brothers, so we almost saw
the paddle sounds grieving arrival
  wet with the last flat slap
  of the cool keel on the bank
  the hand on the thwarts
  with the slow drag of a weightlessness
waiting
we walked where they'd walked
with the cast of our shade
barely proving us there
beside graves, above grass
  above gravel

and the slumberous leaning of stones
later you told me
how in school, you'd slipped indoors
with a loose-limbed girl
how you'd learned
where she was made apple smooth
and sweet as the sea
how she'd let you touch
her second heart
like the dripping of pebbles in wells
for the sacred secret of wishes
and that was your vowelling youth
that parting of limbs
where the best fruit thrives
where the peaches are buxom
and rosy and two to the stem and ten to the branch
and we lost our destination
like still-water wading
up to our voices
in echoes of heaven
while the soul that surrounds us
both talking and silent
is showing the way
to the centre of time.
And this is what loves us
this light and this water
these harlequin maples
these birches tinged silver
these willows all grooming the wind
this sway some are blind to
this phlox in the mauvening mind of the ditch
this wild rose
thrilling the hive hummed heavy with honey

Oh, by all the sad
enthusiasms dulled by aging
say we are alive enough
to wake to this

what reason does the darkness need
but falling
  as we see, and see again
  the simple easing of evening

I say, "you can't be lost
where there's a river ..."
and you laugh
say, "that's profound!"

I say, "pigs want corn"
explain the cribs, the granaries
the markets and the mills
  and how
  the lilies want us
  more than churches
  and what rests in us then
what settles
  and plumbs in the blue
and the black, in the grey
  in the cold and the warm
in the wet and the drear
that mud we were made from
has reasons for rising
  till the beauty of dying
completes us.

(From Dressed in Dead Uncles, *Black Moss Press, 2010)*

VANTAGE

"The absent tree has now become a vantage point."

Alberto Manguel

I start to climb the loss, see there,
I set my foot
where darkness fails to fall, it lifts
the vanished leaf against the light
the *nothing apple* rusted russet in the sun
the coddle wing
that moths about the failing fragrance
of a shadeless shade
I grip at ghosts
and rise like mist in heat
where memory sets heaven
in a bowl of bone—to dream
the morning moon upon the lake is more
and yet
I hold with lessening, I'm fevered
with the feckless ailment of recall
I'm fathered by frail eidolons
made real
and maiden born and spirit crowned
in monumental vapors
like a stone enveiled in fog
old appetites of time
the satiated and eternal past
has passed away in this
unthirsting thing
the roots remain to foil
the shovel face
the broken trunk becomes
a saw-grass vase
the heartwood chokes on sand
the rising dune reclaiming as the wave reclaims its foam

I feel my dust in this encollaring
the hand drift
of a dark caress
the word beyond the sound of words
the limits of a sentient breath
the wind that moves the weather
through the world
it seeks the leaf to shake
green volumes of its living voice
but where the voiceless stoma curl
to palm the dryness of the rain
suspended in the up draw
of a traceless blue
I find the whispering refusal to be gone
and take my nutriment from that
and lean my ladder
on the evening and the dawn

(From In the Muddy Shoes of Morning, *Hidden Brook Press, 2010)*

LAST EVENING

Poem composed after the most recent lunar eclipse sitting on the hill overlooking Long Point Bay, Port Dover

we sat on the hill
overlooking the bay
and watched, keeping vigil
for the full promise
of a total lunar eclipse
the first of its kind in over thirty years
and we were anticipating how the moon
would vanish, darkening down
like the slow sliding over
of an optic lens
blurring the white circle
turning it blood orange
as it is with the fade of lamp glow
burning through gossamer autumn scrim
but here it was
a night of overcast
only a black-veiled widow visage
of reflected light visibly
piercing thin weather
blazing brilliant
through cloud gap
and then gone ghostly grey in vaporous
sweeps of wet web
we lost all hope of stars
in that gothic regard
for we were shrinking down to nothing
but a tree and a dog
and a man and a woman
seated together
in a pair of fan-backed Adirondack chairs
listening to willow whisper of a close at hand breeze
and the loud hush of the lake waves churning

__John B. Lee__ is the Poet Laureate of the city of Brantford in perpetuity and Poet Laureate of Norfolk County for life. Born and raised on a Centennial farm in Kent County southwestern Ontario, among the over eighty prestigious writing awards in 2007, he received the inaugural "Souwesto Award," in recognition for work reflecting the ethos of Southwestern Ontario. He has traveled widely in every province of Canada, and in the summer of 1998 he received the Order of Arctic Adventurers for having walked the Weasel River valley crossing north of the Arctic Circle. He lives in a lake house overlooking Long Point Bay in Port Dover.

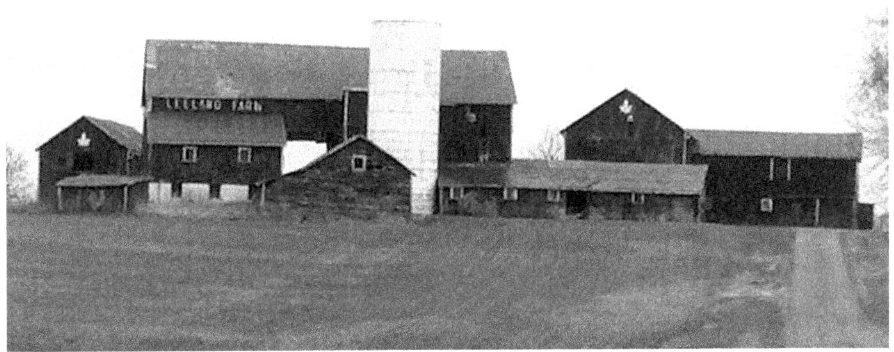

Family Farmhouse in Southwest Ontario by John B. Lee

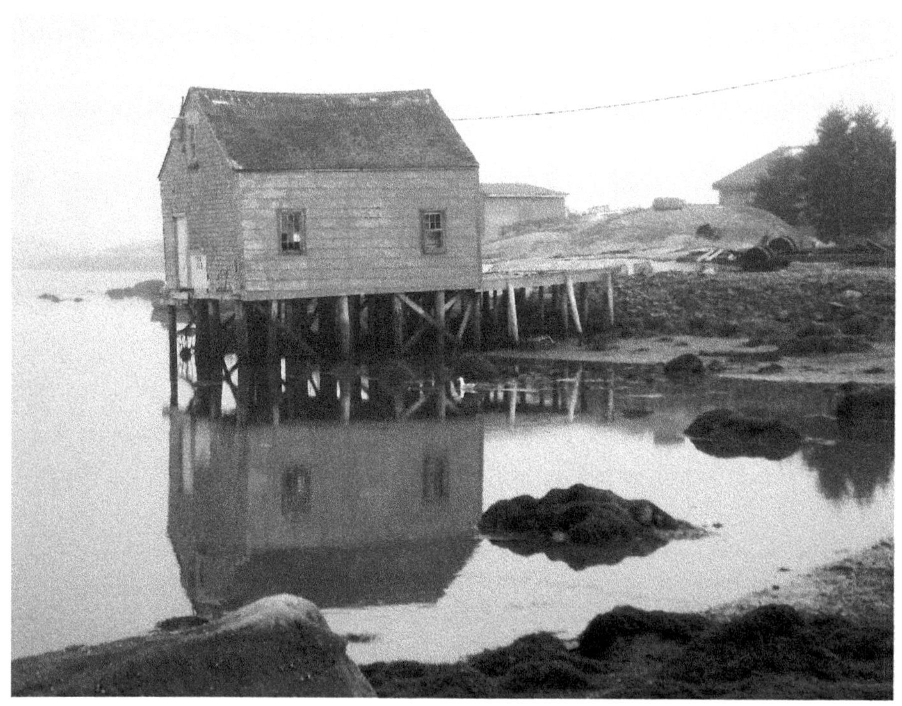

Prospect Point Nova Scotia by Nina Munteanu

I. B. Iskov

CANDLE LIGHTING

I am self-taught in the art
of memorized magic
ancient incantations
ignite in a moment
bloom at once
bright yellow flickering petals
spike halos
run off into the air

My grandmother would be honoured
again and again
lighting her candlesticks
praying respectfully
with mellowed hands
weighted with worries
beneath salt water and scars

My Hebrew is a pretense
I have created myself
wrapped in a Canadian shawl
on a dead end street
moving lips in moral denial

A thick fabric of warmth
shades precious
still

(From Sapphire Seasons, *Aeolus House, 2010)*

CATTLE COUNTRY

They herd toward high ground.
Buffalo, grizzled and bent, are refugees
wandering sacrificial badlands.
Stars could not eclipse the drifting
on an empty sea of terrain,
delicate clouds touch and die.

Thunderous winter winds blow half-insane.

In the midst of Creation,
the bison journey on the pulse of Nature's soul
like naked nomads without an oasis
braving muscled, aching wind-tossed prairies.

Rumpled leaden images rend sharp distances
while some almighty hand slaps
the empty air with rage.

The unofficial history:
Bloated figures nibble on the surface of time.

Reckless gray freedom of the bison
is barbed by silence pure and pale.
Beneath the remote endangered sky,
they welcome the wake of day.

(From Cherish Our Heritage – Recueil bilinge de poésie, *HMS Press, 2004)*

HIGHWAY ELEVEN

I savour a small sliver of Ontario
between Huntsville and Haileybury.

The sweetness of quiet country air,
the freshness of unblemished land;
throngs of trees and grassy fields
blend with occasional wood cabins,
farm houses and road signs.

I wish I could take this all home with me
and place everything outside
my condominium window
to admire every day

instead of the smelly traffic,
over-bearing high-rise buildings
and unending city noise
that congregate and jam
every nook and cranny
of Yonge Street,
where the landscape
of highway eleven
is completely different.

LOOKING IRISH

Growing up, I considered myself Canadian.

My unorthodox family never observed rituals
except when it came to me
dating non-Jewish boys.

I was told they could only be my friends.

Of course, the only time I was invited out
on a date, was by a goy –
a cute one, too.

I spoke my sadness
with solemn sophistication,
explaining I was only allowed to date
nice Jewish boys.

The response was always the same:
"You don't look Jewish."
The funny thing was, when I asked
"What do I look like?"
The response was *still* always the same.

And to think I wasn't even wearing green.

(From Sapphire Seasons, *Aeolus House, 2010)*

MARTIN'S LAND

Familiar archetypes shade the day.

The cool smoothness of the evening breeze
escapes ageing green.

Tiny skeletons capture a moonbeam,
paint copper on twigs.

Each wind-scattered seed grows
a careless inventory
thrust deep into wet firmament.

The desolate row on row
of ancient wooded towers
numbs aching ground.

The rhythm of waving grass
and the distant song of a lone owl
harmonize in this familiar country setting.

Martin surveys his land
in small-town Ontario.

(From Martin's History, *Beret Days Press, 2013)*

WHERE IS SHE?

Half-smiling, a young woman stands in sepia tones,
her light brown hair coiffed like Garbo's.

My mother, in her better memory, confessed:
This is my sister, Basha. She was my father's favourite.
Isn't she beautiful?

My sixteen-year-old brain racing,
I wondered why
my mother never told me
about this other auntie,
about her husband,
my other uncle
and their two daughters,
my other cousins.

I wondered why
I never got to visit them
and why my mother's parents never mentioned
this important person,
their eldest and most attractive, intelligent daughter,
all the years they lived in Canada
after the war.

I looked at my mother, full of questions
and asked only one:
Where is she?

My mother, wiping tears, blurted:
She was murdered by the Nazis
with her husband and children.

(From The Passover Literary Supplement of The Canadian Jewish News, *March, 2013. Also in* Skirting the Edge, *IOWI, 2015)*

ONTARIO IN THE SPRING

If you take a trip through Ontario
in April, May or June,
the morning dew and sunshine
will sing their country tune.

Farmland stretches to the sun
with quilted patchwork soil.
Cows and horses quietly graze
while farmers daily toil.

Century homes are nestled
in little towns along the way.
The balconies and gumwood trim
are a part of the display.

Bed and Breakfasts and quaint motels
wait patiently to greet you.
Friendly folks with hometown jokes
are always glad to meet you.

The highway's a silver ribbon
securely wrapped around the terrain.
It leads you on a memorable tour
And then back home again.

(From After The Rain, *Snowapple Press, 2001)*

TESTING THE WATERS

(In memory of Heine Mondrowitz, who drowned on Lake Nippissing on Aug. 21, 2006)

It is not hard for me
to remember you
scanning uncharted territory.

Others, far less adventurous,
stood land-locked at dance-floor edge,
while music flowed anxious and free.

At twelve, I had only started to develop
a love for music and dancing
and you my first crush glided
across the endless sea of grey-blue floor
and asked me to dance.

Sadie Hawkins would have been proud.
It was my day and hers.
When you sailed me
around and around,
judges were pointing
and gave us high marks for showmanship.

As our ship reversed, we twisted in open water.
I think this happened when you died.
You spun around and around on a windy axis,
burned into sunlight, and sailed away to heaven.

(From Sapphire Seasons, *Aeolus House, 2010)*

THE CULTURE OF NATIVE ART

Hidden amongst skyscrapers
and monster high-rise glass buildings,
in shadowy recesses sprinkled throughout North America,
an ancestral connection initiated by Haida carvers
still prevails.

Beginning with the birth of the raven,
expressions of beauty were carved with romantic energy,
tinged with darkness out of loneliness and alienation.

Extraordinary acts of faith
displayed on old poles in native villages
are punctuated by songs of Manitou.
Massive totem parks and museums
in no smooth patterns,
conserve and protect the mythical
in a vanished heritage.

The eagle and the bear reside comfortably
in a large clamshell.
Boxwood maple totem poles
conceal their homes intricately.

Order and control cannot prevent the raven
from stealing the limelight.
Stretched to the limit,
a broken beak turns out quirky surprises.
Gravity-bound,
matter and spirit rise
to challenge time and change.

There is an aura of sentiment
and an aching nostalgia connected to the art,
making it monumental.

(From Skirting the Edge, *IOWI, 2015)*

THE SEA CADET

At fifteen, Martin was restless.
He gave up smoking.
He was no youngster.

He was ready for the crisp white uniform,
master the secret of how to untie the knot.

He knew he could go far –
as far as Halifax, anyway.

He watched the sun-sparkle on ocean waves,
never concerned
some gale could lift and carry him off.

He was stalwart.

He climbed the ship's ladder of success.
At twenty, he was an officer,
feared and revered by the younger cadets.

At the social,
all were too scared
to ask his pretty sister for a dance.

(From Martin's History, *Beret Days Press, 2013)*

THE TRUCKER ON THE 401

Roadie in red shirt, black hat, yellow
teeth and fingers
rides the lane
noisy rollicking steamroller
will not be swayed.

Sashays down the highway
flicking sardonic ashes
under exalted wheels
with savoir faire.

Pulls away
my thoughts   trail
smoke and exhaust
rise in chorus
sing to the cumbrous sawhorse
cutting up the road.

In the common calamity of road rage,
hurled rocks, guns and hunting knives,
the trucker on the 401
rolled up
shirtsleeves and windows
continues to drive with reckless abandon.

(From Henry's Creature: Poems and Stories on the Automobile, *Black Moss Press, 2000)*

I.B. (Bunny) Iskov *is the Founder of The Ontario Poetry Society www.theontariopoetrysociety.ca. Her work has been published in several literary journals and anthologies. She has three full collections and lots of chapbooks. In 2009, Bunny was the recipient of the inaugural R.A.V.E. Award, Recognizing Arts Vaughan Excellence in recognition of outstanding contribution to the cultural landscape of the City of Vaughan. The award is for Art Educator / Mentor in the Literary Arts.*

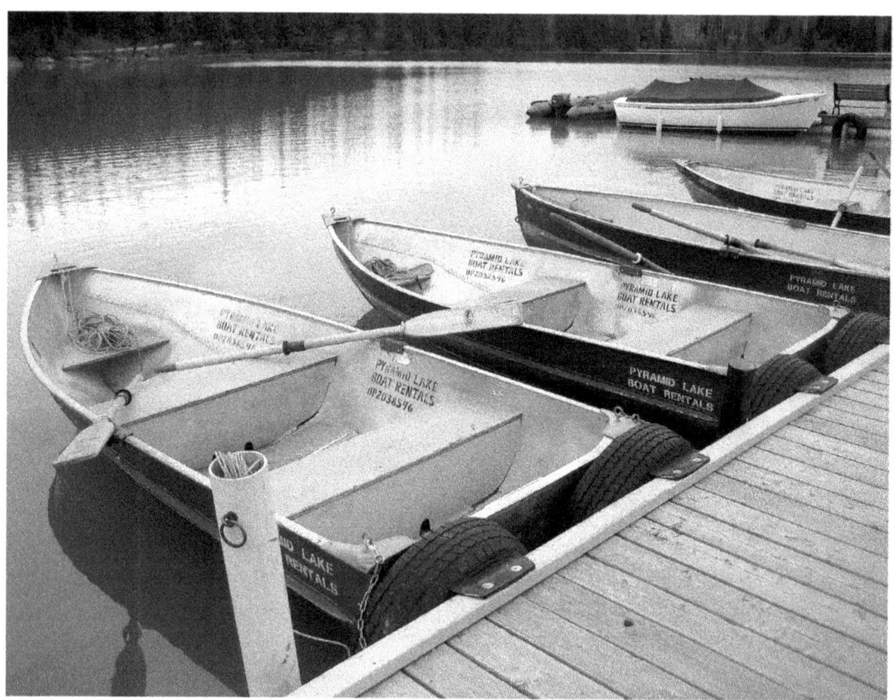

Banff Boats by Kumkum Ramchandani

Jasmine Jackman

QANIK[1]

White pristine land of hidden jewels
Dotted with *inuksuit*[2] guiding men back
From the hunt laden with precious gifts.
The glow of the *kudlik*[3] beckons hunters home,
With each step *maujag*[4] buries feet like quicksand.
Aputi[5] mounds around the igloo lit by the hearth within.
The whine of dogs carries on mournful wind
Joined by the howling of wolves in the midst.
The scent of burning whale blubber and moss
Filters through the igloo
And away into bracing, frigid Arctic air.
The family huddles over cooking pots as *aniu*[6] melts.
The wind whistles wildly around the igloo
While women hang clothes to dry
Seeking warmth from the family fire
Listening as the men beguile their captive audience
With the story of the hunt.

---

1 Falling snow in the Inuktitut dialect of Nunavik
2 Plural of Inuksuk; manmade stone landmarks
3 Oil lamp used by the Inuit
4 The snow in which one sinks
5 The snow on the ground
6 Snow used to make water

LAND OF THE MIDNIGHT SUN

Barren tundra butts upon the northern boreal forest
of opulent green
birthed from the sweet water delta
where majestic ranges tower over
a spider web of lakes and streams
home to hardy flora and fauna
creating passageways to remote habitations
unknown adventures
leading to the "place of people."[1]

1 Inuvik, a town in the Northwest Territories

THE IMMIGRANT

You leave home to find your wealth
Across the mountains and then the seas.
You promise to write every day.
Don't get lost.

You make your way
Slowly, timidly,
Make new friends and learn their ways.
Now you write less frequently.
Don't get lost.

News from you comes regularly — Facebook, Twitter and email.
You promise to return after your studies, but instead
You find a girl and land a job,
You learn to speak,
You hide your heritage from all you meet.
Don't get lost.

Never you mind, you say,
No need to return because I will send for you.
I will help you make your way.
Your news comes sporadically.
Don't get lost.

A month, two months and then a year go by and no news from you,
Only pictures and links of information from friends.
You have made a new life for yourself.
Your family back home is now but a faint memory.
Your adopted country is what you choose.
Don't get lost.

And then the tap runs dry.
No more news comes from you.
Although we know your address
You are lost *to us.*

THE TRAVELLERS

I had to rub my eyes.
A black woman and Asian man holding hands.
But wait, the shine off her hand says they're married.

I spied them in the Tuileries Garden
Sitting and feeding the geese
While gladly taking pictures of families that asked.
What are they on? Why are they so content?

Then, I ended up behind them in line at the bank
And when they reached the wicket
The teller closed her window
Pointing to the clock that showed closing time.
Ferme!
No problem, they said, we will be back tomorrow at ten.
Whilst I was mad as hell;
With no cash for the evening
I would be forced to stay in.

As we left the bank, the rain fell.
Merde!
The rain wet my new suede jacket
I tried to shelter from the deluge
Turned my jacket inside out.
The couple lifted their eyes to the sky
Then like Fred Astaire and Ginger Rogers …
Danced away hand in hand
Laughing and singing in the rain.

A while later, I met them again at the hotel.
This time, my room key wouldn't work
And just as I was about to lose it
They opened up their room to me
So as to call the hotel clerk
And avoid the four-flight trip back to reception.
They offered me wine to calm my nerves.

I looked around their room
Saw coloured "paper" on the desk —
Purple, green, red, and brown. Strange money.
Ah, now it makes sense —
They must be from out of town.
I spied a flag tagged to their luggage …
Red and white
They are from the land of lakes and maple syrup.
Of course! The politeness, the kindness
The patience —
They are Canadian!

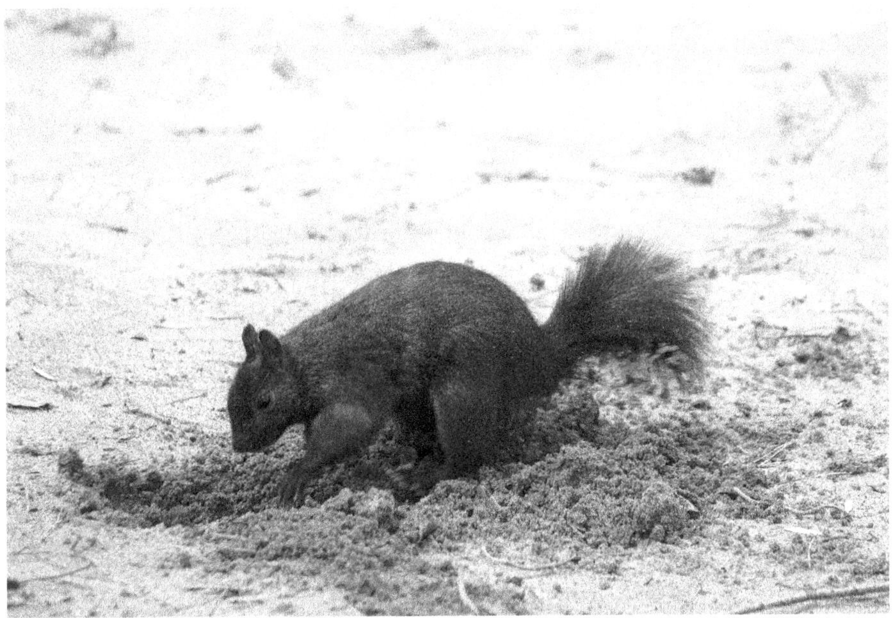

Black Squirrel Digging by Merridy Cox-Bradley

CLOSE CALL

Connor had been sitting at the bar since the house party began. The basement was filled with friends from his school. The speakers blared, the noise was deafening and Connor's ears were ringing. He glanced at his watch — it was already 10:30 pm. He was convinced by now that his girlfriend Debbie wasn't coming — she had never been two hours late before.

"Hey man!" Rob said sitting down next to Connor at the bar, reaching for a soft drink and wiping the sweat off his forehead. This was the first time in two hours that he had taken a break. "You gonna sit there all night or are you going to get up and dance?" Rob poked as he pirouetted around Connor like James Brown.

"Naw, I'm gonna wait for Deb. She said she'd be here."

"I hate to point out the obvious, man. But, if she is not here by now, then she ain't comin'," Rob teased. Then, a woman appeared out of the crowd and pulled Rob back to the dance floor. Marvin Gaye's song *Let's Get It On* brought everyone to their feet.

Connor, in an act of desperation, looked around the room. All the spaces along the wall were taken up and a few unfortunate souls danced aimlessly in the middle of the dance floor under the disco light, while the couples along the wall practically made love to each other through their clothes. The smell of cigarettes, sweat and cheap perfume hung in the air.

Connor felt his leg vibrate. He pulled out his cell. Five missed calls — starting from 8:30 pm — and one text, all from Debbie. "Crap," he moaned.

Rob returned to the bar after the song had finished and gulped down the last of his soft drink; as the DD he wasn't drinking alcohol tonight.

"Listen," Connor yelled over the music into Rob's ear. "I have to go to Deb's. Her parents are away for the night celebrating their 25th anniversary and she had to stay home to babysit her younger sister and brother. I'll get Deb to give me a ride home."

"Alright," Rob said evilly, "You lucky skunk! I want to hear all about it tomorrow!"

"You know a gentleman never kisses and tells," Connor replied, slyly making his way to the stairs, awkwardly brushing by couples making out on his way out.

After leaving the party, Connor made his way down the long, winding road that led past the train yard. The music from the party lessened with every step until all that could be heard was a faint bass. It was abnormally warm for the middle of the night in December. Well, that was the Alberta winters — one day you were in shorts, the next in parkas and it was 40 below. Connor was happy he had dressed for the weather. His beige cotton golf pants and white oxford shirt breathed, although he sported no hat or gloves.

The evening sky shone a kaleidoscope of pale green, red and pink lights that draped across the sky, fading away and reappearing. It was particularly beautiful tonight. Connor began to slow down, mesmerized. And then he felt a tap on his head and another.

"Bloody hell!" he yelled, as the raindrops increased in size and fell heavily. He went from a trot to a jog and then a full out sprint as he ran for cover. With at least another thirty minutes on foot to walk, Connor wondered if he should turn back and seek refuge at the party and forget about Debbie. But he remembered that her parents were away for the night — this may be his last chance to get to third base with her. Upon closer inspection, Connor found that there was a hole in the fence. People must have been using it to take a shortcut through the train yard to get to the street on the other side saving a good forty minutes. Periodically, people used the slow-moving trains to hitch a ride home. That was one thing Connor hated about living so far north — no public transit. Even though the police were cracking down on trespassers, nothing was going to deter Connor from seeing Debbie tonight. He was soaked through to the bone and, despite the warm temperatures, was feeling quite chilled.

Emboldened by his circumstances, Connor opted to take a shortcut to Debbie's house. He darted through the fence, nicking his shoulder on the metal hanging from the fence. He could feel the warm blood running down his back, but he was determined to cross the tracks without being seen by security and hop on a slow-moving freight train going in his direction. There were so many trains, and Connor wasn't sure which one to take. He settled on the Redpath train because he had seen it go past Debbie's house many times. The train could get him to Debbie's a lot faster than walking, so he ran alongside of the train and jumped on. Now out of the rain, bedraggled and tired, Connor tended to his wound.

He enjoyed the scenery as familiar houses and stores floated by under the shimmering lights of the aurora borealis. He briefly thought about jumping off the train; however, he liked the feel of the warm air slapping his face and the peaceful rest he was enjoying. He decided to stay on the train until it got just a little closer to Debbie's neighbourhood. Then, all of a sudden, the train geared up even more. The shift in gears almost knocked Connor off the train. It was moving so quickly now that Connor could barely hold his head up. He slinked over hugging the floor and wall until he got to the end of the car. Perched between two rail cars, he prepared to make his move. Except it was too late, the train was going too fast for him to jump off safely.

"Shit!" He was stuck outside. As he contemplated his fate, he saw Debbie's house flash by and then disappear into the night until all that was left was the dim glow of the town lights in the distance. He reached for his cell phone. The train was moving so fast, he had to be careful not to let it fly out of his hands. He had 10 percent battery power left. The temperature had plummeted so quickly that his hands were ice cold, and he couldn't dial a number. Fortunately, Debbie's number was on speed dial. One ring … another … and then another. "Pick up the bloody phone!" Connor yelled desperately. The answering machine came on. Connor was just about to hang up when he heard, "Heellloo?"

Connor sighed, "Deb, thank God! It's me! I'm stuck on the Redpath train and I can't —"

A little voice interrupted, "What you doing on the train? That train isn't for people, silly!" It was Debbie's younger sister, Shelly, who just turned 5.

"Oh, my God, Shelly, please get Debbie on the phone NOW!" Connor pleaded.

"Debbie's putting Johnny to bed," Shelly snapped. "I'm not going to talk to you if you are going to yell."

The line went dead. Connor cursed like he had never cursed before. The train was going very fast now and he could barely make out the houses from the trees. The wind cut his eyes like shards of glass. He squinted at his phone. There was barely a bar of juice left. In sheer panic, he hit the emergency dial for 911.

"Yes, what is your emergency?" Connor blurted out his name and address, and then there was a loud train whistle that seemed to go on forever; he tried to tell the operator through the noise what had happened but the phone went dead. Connor whipped his phone out into the blackness in frustration, immediately sorry that he had done that.

Within minutes, Connor was out in the wilderness with no landmarks to tell him where he was. The temperature began to drop rapidly. Frightened, Connor held tightly to the metal of the freight train that began to freeze to his bare hands as the train journeyed deeper into the cold prairie night.

Even with the adrenaline pumping through his veins, he was freezing. "This is pretty serious," Connor started to think. "I could freeze to death."

As the temperature continued to drop, Connor started to lose feeling in his limbs. Just as he was losing all hope of ever being rescued, he remembered that his parents would be devastated and probably blame themselves if he died. He had to do whatever he could to live. He started to chant "I want to live" over and over. He didn't waste his energy screaming for help as he could see that he was on the second-last car of at least fifteen. No one would ever hear him in this desolate landscape. His throat started drying up from the cold air — even the tears on his eyelashes started to form crystals. It seemed as if the Northern Lights were mocking him as they danced a beautiful ballet, pulsating with alternating wisps of colours. He felt himself floating up to take his place among the stars — and then everything went black.

Connor heard some noise and slowly opened his eyes. "He's up!" he heard someone shout.

His mother sobbed, "Oh, my god! We thought we'd lost you!"

Could this have been a dream? He felt like Dorothy in *The Wizard of Oz*. He was back in his home town — in the hospital. His parents were sitting on either side of him at a hospital bed. His girlfriend, Debbie, was leaning over him.

"How did you find me?" Connor asked quizzically.

Debbie's voice cracked as she tried to hold back her tears. "Well, after you called, Shelly was going on about how rude you had been to her and fortunately your conversation was recorded on the answering machine, so I contacted the police and gave them your cell number so that they could trace your cell signal.

"You were found barely clinging to life. In fact, it was a miracle you didn't fall off the train because when they found you, you were hypothermic, semi-conscious and severely frostbitten." Then Debbie's tone changed. "I just have to ask you one thing." She paused, staring intently in his eyes, then began shouting, "Were you out of your fricking mind!!!? Whatever possessed you to hop on a freight train!?"

Connor replied sheepishly, "It was only supposed to be for a few blocks." He broke down and cried. He tried to hug Debbie but his hands were bandaged.

His dad just hugged Connor tightly. Connor could feel his dad's tears rolling down his neck. "Well, you'll be spending more time at home working off the $2500 fine for trespassing," his father finally managed to squeak out through his strained vocal cords. His tears messed up Connor's hair.

Connor thought the fine and the possibility that he might lose a few fingers to frostbite were a small price to pay for another chance at life. He had survived a very close call.

(Based on a true story from a news article: http://www.cbc.ca/news/canada/edmonton/near-frozen-man-not-a-train-hopper-1.827088)

Jasmine Jackman *was born in England and immigrated to Canada with her West Indian parents and siblings when she was three years old. She currently resides in Mississauga, Ontario. An advocate for social justice, Jasmine sits on several community boards, including: Writers and Editors Network, United Nations Association of Canada Toronto Region, Skills for Change, Bridging the Gap, and RISE Up! Rise ABOVE! She is a member of the Canadian Ethnic Media Association, Canadian Confederation of Poets, and contributor to the Persian Tribune. She is also a recipient of several Teacher Recognition awards. Her poetry and short stories have been published in anthologies and newspapers.*

Anna Yin

LIFE JARS

When I was a child,
I was told
silence is like light,
having colors and faces.

Walking through the country in the dark,
I used to fill a glass jar with fireflies.
It became my green starry compass.
When I inhaled the silence,
I could hear quiet voices from living creatures,
each making music of its own life.

Now grown up,
every day's busy journey in this hectic city,
I thought our life jars must be full of mundane trifles and noises;
Yet wandering into ravines in this urban landscape,
I can find the silence, silence and silence —
Where it opens a door like sunrays breaking through.

Riding along the lakeshore,
I see sunset's serene reflection on the lake,
The Port Credit lighthouse topping its splendor.

A baby swan takes off …
I inhale the silence.

(From Seven Nights with the Chinese Zodiac *Black Moss Press 2015)*

HELLO, CANADA

cool morning air
and crisp birdcalls
kick off this special day

glittering diamonds
roll on a green blanket
children hooray all the way

parade ahead –
cartoon figures from floats
blow kisses and dance along

music far and near …
lilacs scent and sweetness spreads
bubbles from bottles of beer

by the City Hall, the Mayor
waves to cheerful crowds …
our peaceful and welcome world

brushes touch up
flags on fresh faces
… O, Canada … in unison

sun shines candy clouds
carnival at Celebration Square
new and old friends meet

caring for the needy
young and old gather to share
… triple sweet

this is Canada, our Canada
fireworks bloom on night sky
a sound and sweet dream

Note: Anna Yin as Mississauga's Inaugural Poet Laureate wrote this series of haiku and presented it during Mississauga's official ceremony for 2015 Canada Day.

Anna Yin *was born in China and immigrated to Canada in 1999. She has five poetry books and won the 2005 Ted Plantos Memorial Award, the 2010/2014 MARTY Awards and the 2013 Professional Achievement Award from CPAC, etc. Her poems have appeared in Arc Poetry, New York Times, China Daily, CBC, etc. Anna is currently Ontario representative for the League of Canadian Poets and Mississauga's Inaugural Poet Laureate. Her website is annapoetry.com.*

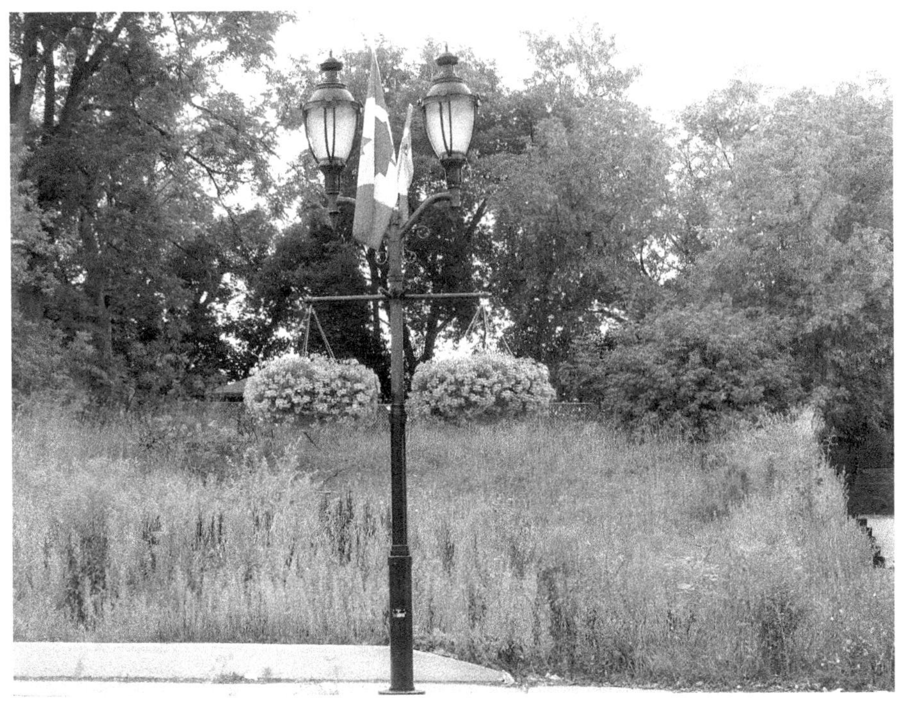

Canadian Flag by Janine Georgiou-Zeck

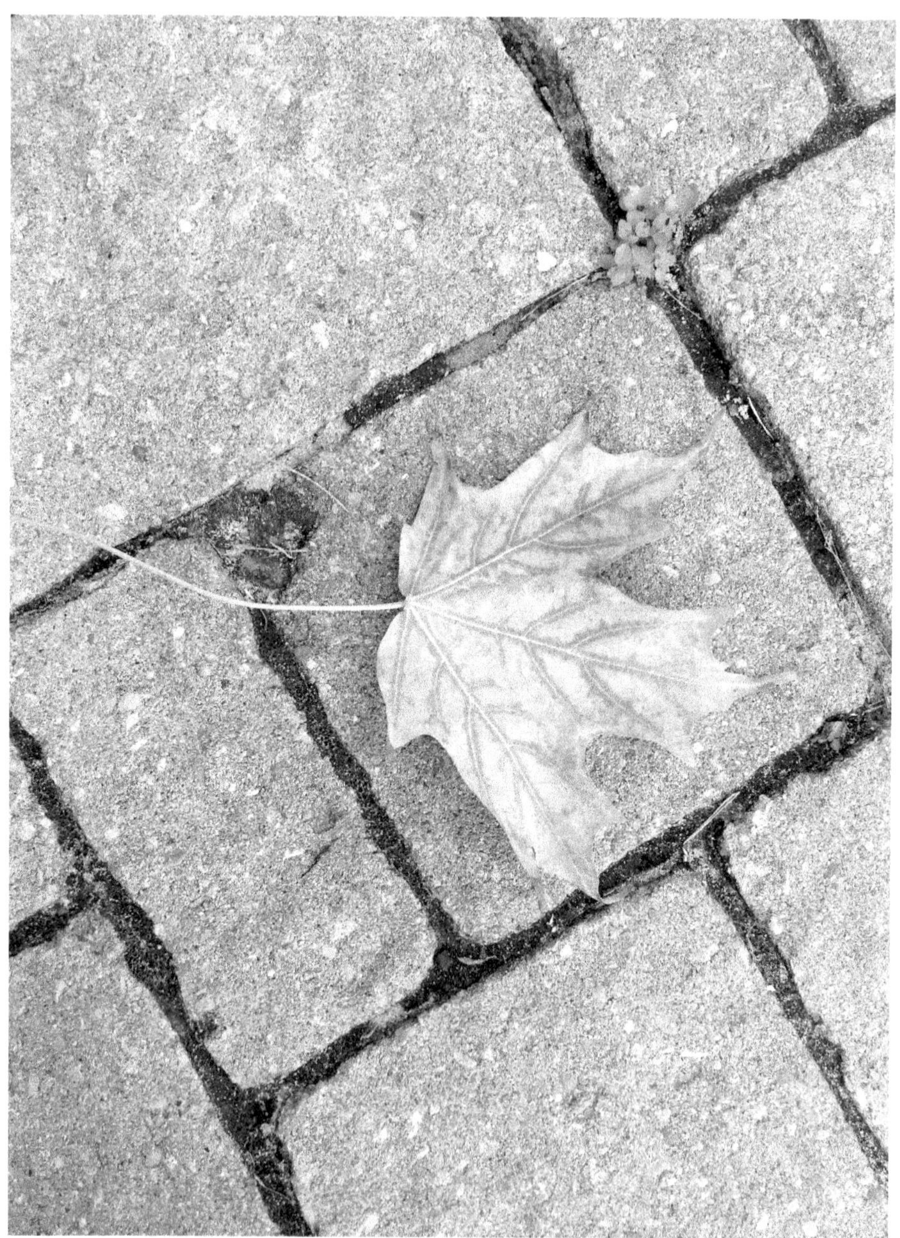

Maple Leaf on Stone Paving by Janine Georgiou-Zeck

Barry Clegg

THIS IS TORONTO

I am a tightpacked staring statistic
clattering and swaying through the ground,
while seated passengers read or squinch eyes
and evade the gallantry of offering seats.
St Clair at last, my stop. The joy of decompression falters
up on the street when I reach for my sunglasses.
Check every pocket, every backpack pouch, each one again
and then again, as the truth sinks in.
Must have dropped them on the subway.
Prescription sunglasses. Hundreds of dollars. And
needed tomorrow for an out-of-town trip.
My name and number are in the case, it comes back to me,
and optimism grants a whiff of comfort.
Nevertheless a gloom settles.
At night, my wife answers the phone. "I'll get my husband."
Then: "Barry, someone called Raymond has good news."
The someone called Raymond has my sunglasses.
I thank him jubilantly, effusively.
We discuss locations, next steps. He lives near the subway
five, six stops away.
"Give me your address, I can drive round right now
to pick them up – if it's not too late."
No, I'll take the subway to St Clair. I have a Metropass,
it will cost me nothing and be easier for you.
In the face of his quiet insistence I concur.
We settle on McDonald's, station entrance, half past ten.
"Right," I say, "I'll be there. I'm wearing a yellow shirt."
And I'm a Chinese guy in a grey sweater.

The night is balmy. I cycle over to St Clair, buy myself
a coffee, and take up position outside McDonald's.

A friend approaches the station. I announce, "I'm waiting for a stranger to bring my sunglasses! Tell you another time…"

An SUV pulls up: the husband goes inside, the wife waits behind the wheel. He struggles back in with two ice-creams.

Across the street is the Library where… But this must be him.

"Raymond?"

Barry!

An assured handshake and he gives me the glasses. I press three ten-dollar bills on him. "Do something nice with this."

He murmurs *Thank you*, not looking down, too polite to refuse.

He might be a surgeon – or a waiter

or an accountant – this rare man who offers no clues.

For all the good will between us, small talk is awkward. "This is wonderfully kind of you."

He sees my helmet. *Do you cycle a lot?*

"Not really, for me the bike's just a vehicle. There it is, locked up with one of those kryptonite U-bars."

That should do the trick!

"Hope so. The last time I stood outside McDonald's, I actually saw a man cut the cable lock from my old bike – it was over there by the Library – and ride off on it."

Did you stop him?

"I dropped my milkshake and ran like hell, but couldn't catch him. Never saw the bike again."

Raymond shakes his head. *That's Toronto*, he says.

But I rap him on the arm with my spectacle case. "No, this is Toronto, Raymond."

I wave it before his eyes. "*This* is Toronto!"

We smile like old friends.

***Barry Clegg** is an engineer with an MA from Cambridge University and an MSc in Solid Mechanics from Aston University. He worked as an engineer in England before moving to Toronto in 1969, and spent over 30 years in software development and IT management. He is now a freelance communicator in Toronto, and working on his third book of poetry. His published books are* A Rare Spectacle *(2010) and* The Beginning of Time *(2013).*

Merridy Cox-Bradley

THEOLOGY

One day, on an old Toronto trolley,
My schoolfriend asked me about—
God.
I told her how I once met Him,
Not in a traditional church but
On a hill of soft grasses and flowers—
A sunny slope just far enough
For solitude, under a maple tree,
Warmed by a southern breeze.
White clouds scudded by like woolly sheep.
Here I felt a lively spirit enter
In an all-encompassing peace and joy,
Settling into my heart the knowledge
Of freedom, whispering: *That I Am.*

But, at fifteen, I was not convincing,
And my friend said: God is an old man
With a long beard, who lives in a cloud,
And she definitely did not believe—
God.

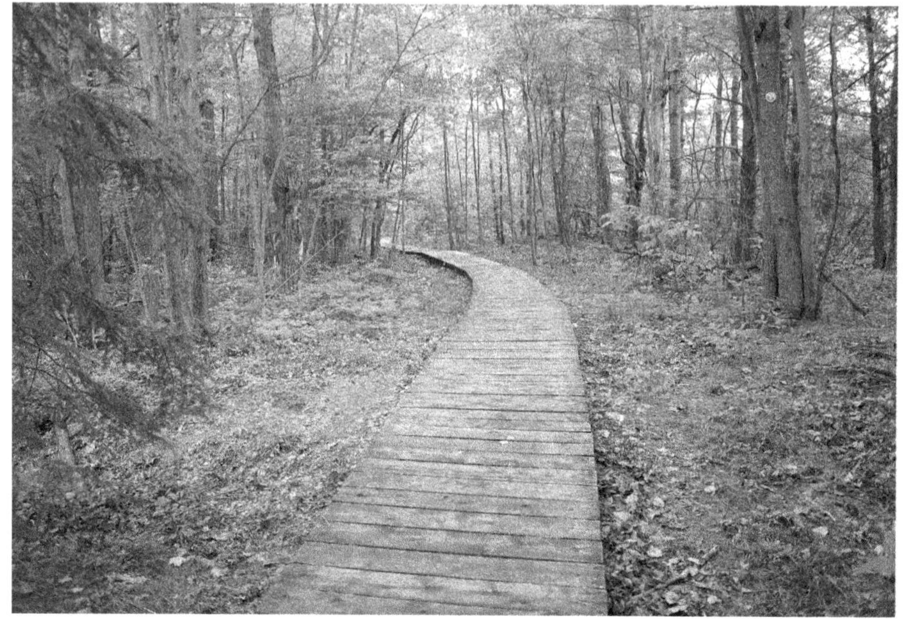

Boardwalk Through Forest by Merridy Cox-Bradley

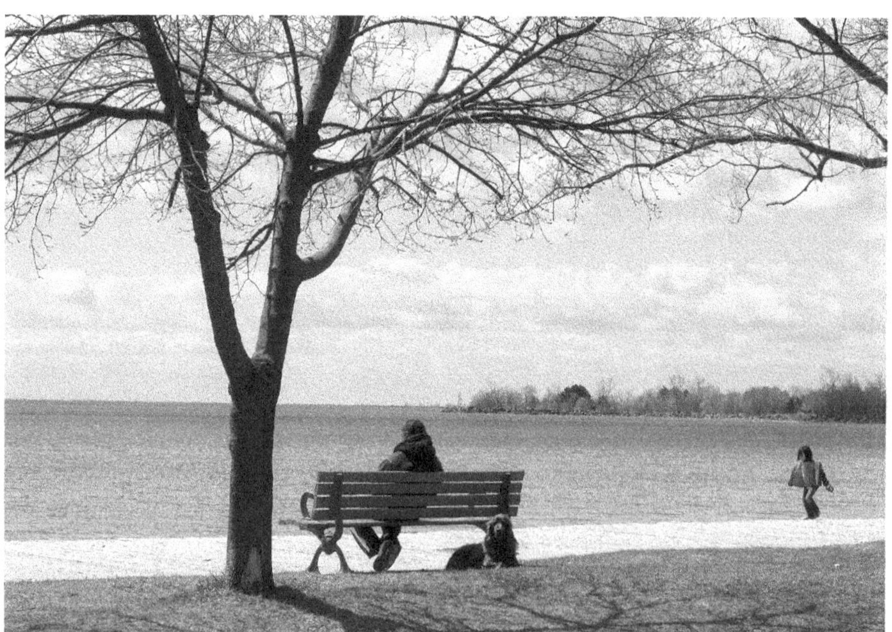

Relaxing by the Lake by Merridy Cox-Bradley

THE POND

In Caledon, along an old railway line,
Now a green forest trail,
Quietly I walk as
The sun warms the earth.
I look for spring flowers and
Songbirds returning from the south.
Water runs off the bank
And soaks the path there
Where I must watch my feet and
Step over roots of encroaching cedars.
Quite hidden is the pond
Where the hills form a cup
And the rocks create a ledge
I can sit on for a while.
This place is magical,
Where secret water
Shelters salamanders
And their clusters of eggs,
Where red efts roam the verge
And blackbirds claim the rushes,
Where ferns unfurl fisted fronds.
Here I sit, watching all as
The sun warms the silence.
Finally, Nature reveals
New growth before my eyes.
I stand, the ancient rock
Solid beneath my feet,
Stretch out and breathe in
The vibrancy of newness
And spring growth in the air.
Silent, standing, open-hearted,
What I embrace as if new
Is an old, old wisdom
Of connectivity.

NIAGARA ESCARPMENT FOREST

I stand deep in the forest,
Feeling deep underwater.
The treetops crash above me,
Like rolling waves on the sea.
The gale, only a gust down here,
Swirls the treetops in mad circles.
The branches groan and moan,
Leaves sound out a low rustling.
Tall tree trunks catch my soul.
To look up at the sway, the swirls
Is dizzying, giddying.
Where are the songbirds lurking?
Can they ride the stormy trees?
The wind howling through branches,
At once exhilarating,
All but obliterating
My ordinary thoughts of
Indoor, man-made, still places.
A near branch cracks
And crashes down to the ground.
My trance breaks, and like the birds,
I yearn to hide safe away.
I'm for home, for silences;
I'm for hot tea and supper,
But I carry the forest,
Tall and rolling, in my soul.

MYTH VS. REALITY

Canada has a dearth of mythical beasts:
No leprechauns, as you might find in Ireland,
No Scandinavian gnomes, except in ads.
The Loch Ness monster may not be over there
But neither has it migrated over here.
Lovely unicorns do not grace our woods,
Although, there is a serious search on
For the great Northern Dancer's double,
Even though that is but a race horse.
Bigfoot has been sighted in various spots,
Abominable though he may be, and
If he could be well and truly captured,
He would likely say "Sasquatch" and disappear.
We have lost that old trickster, Whiskey Jack,
Who now pretends to be a mere grey jay
Or perhaps, on occasion, a coyote
And, in truth, we are the poorer for that.
We are mostly now sophisticated
City dwellers, so detached from Nature
That we might not even recognize
A real beast, should it run across our path:
A fox, say, or a marten, or a weasel.
We look for the myths that were never there,
While the reality of our wild beasts
Is dwindling, obscured by bright lights,
Run out of town by back hoes and asphalt trucks.

When Europeans finally discover
Canada over here, they demand to see
Wolverines, elk, muskox or buffalo,
And we have to admit that, while we slept,
Whole populations of wolves, bear and deer
Were relegated to mythical status.
Beavers became tall hats, elk were lost for oil,
Buffalo have morphed into spicy wings,
Coyotes are now coats (at least the odd time).

We don't want those wild things in our way here,
Assuming that they're still there in the north
And available for tourists, of course.

Why do we search for the mythical beast,
Blindly missing the real, magical ones?
What is city infrastructure, after all,
Without the foundation of ecology?
Even in the city, our lives rely on
Nature for our sustenance and our souls.
The Beasts, mythical or not, are saying
You cannot live in just a concrete world.

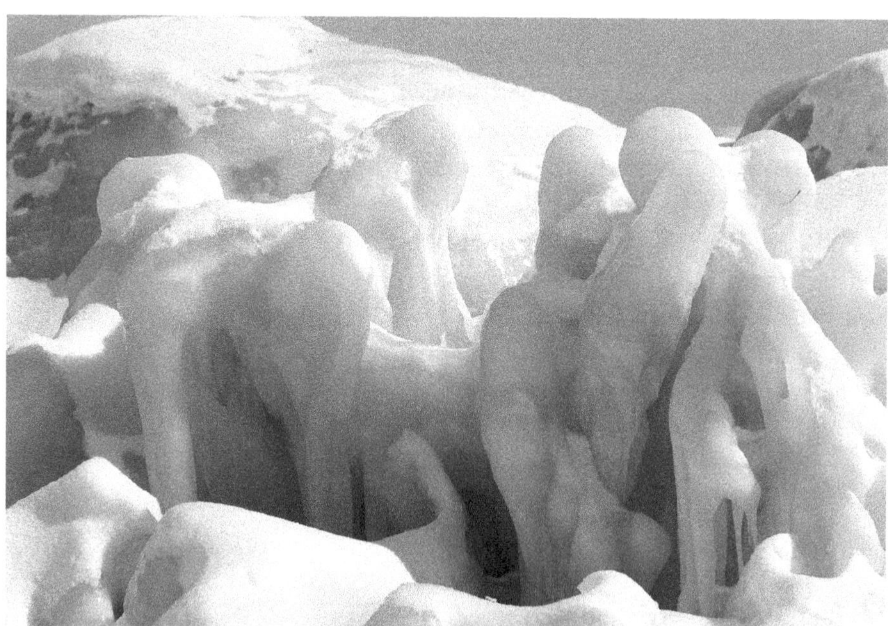

Snow Ghosts by Merridy Cox-Bradley

LANDMARK TREES DOWN IN THE BACK FORTY

Down in the back forty[1]
There is a copse of trees
Spared by the lumbermen
Because they were stunted
By the rocks they grew amidst.
These trees, large and wide, were
Riddled by ants and grubs,
Hollowed out by woodpeckers
And water. Broken branches
Created space for nests
Of squirrels and owlets.
Gnarly boles grew like brains
Clinging to the trunks,
And, indeed, these trees have
Intelligence because
They survived the men
Who cut the forest down.
Their wisdom branches out
To show us the way we
Ought to go from now on.

Down in the back forty
There is a copse of trees,
A good destination
For an afternoon walk.
There are grandmother trees
That have seeded the land
With new trees growing strong,
Reaching for the Lanark sky.
I'm drawn to these trees,
Inevitably drawn,
Because they speak to me
Of landscape and longing.
As landmark trees, they help
To show us the way we
Ought to go from now on.

Down in the back forty
There is a copse of trees,
Stunted, riddled, broken,
Hollowed out, misshapen—
But only here can be
Found Life teeming, growing,
Being, flying, nesting—
Just to show us how we
Ought to go from now on.

Down in the back forty
There is a copse of trees
That will listen to you
If you go and sit for awhile
And tell them how you feel
Stunted, riddled, broken,
Hollowed out, misshapen—
And they will show you how
To inspire others
To be and grow …
And they will show us how we
Ought to go from now on.

1 "Back forty"originally referred to the back 40 acres of a hundred-acre farm, which was usually undeveloped land.

FOREST GLADE

There are glades in the forest,
Patches of soft grasses,
Some so inaccessible
That fairies are free to play
Around tiny daisy Maypoles.
Other glades are sunlit spots
Where I can hide with a book—
The access path is hidden—
A deer may have lain there last
Leaving a round indentation
The shape of its whole body
Where it curled in the grass.

The beauty is that no one
Knows the guilty joy I have
To steal time, book in hand,
Sweet uninterrupted time,
For fantasy and hero,
Character, setting and plot.
But then, the sunny setting
And the shade of the big trees
Carries my soul away in
A trance of beauty and joy,
Shakespearean and present,
Punctured by whistling birds
And the rustle of beetles:
Those creatures who own the glade
And the ecology there.

On a hot, sunny day,
I mark my page with a leaf,
Put my book down on a rock
And take up Imagination:
Perhaps, the glade will reveal
Its own secrets, joys, and tales.

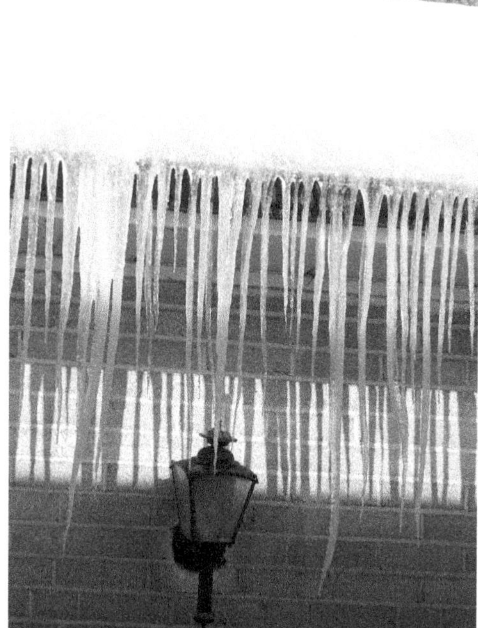

Icicles by Merridy Cox-Bradley

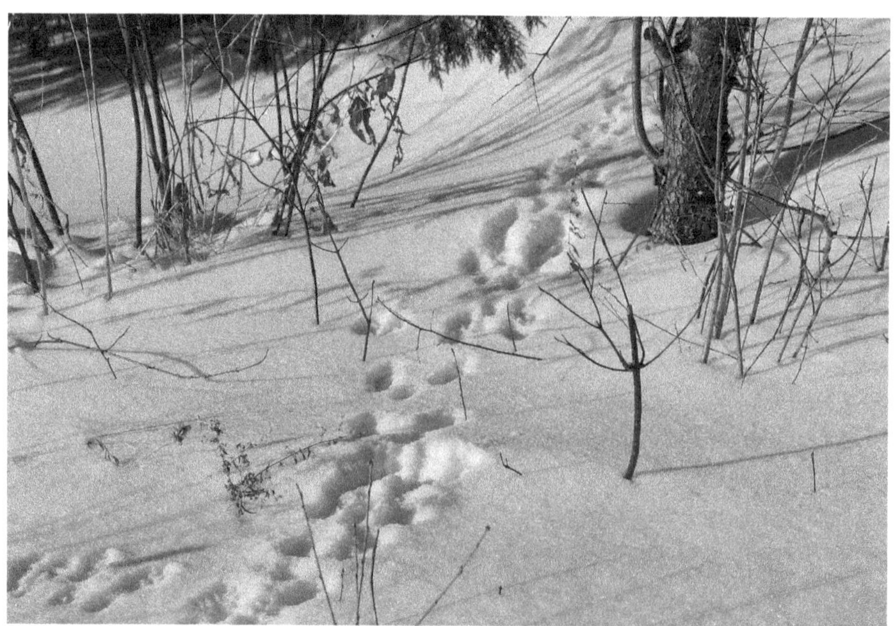

Bunny Prints in the Snow by Merridy Cox-Bradley

CLIFF AND AERIE

On the steep hillside there is a good place
Where you can look down into the valley
And watch the sun rising from the hill's crease
To the pink sky of a summer morning.
Over the treetops glide the tippy great
Raptors—bare-headed vultures, impressive
As they circle the updrafts of the hills
And the grand sky, in their own element.
I stood there once and studied the great birds,
As they patrolled the valley below.
Can you follow flying things, where they go?

Across the valley was a cliff obscured
Almost by trees and there the vultures went—
And so did I, first walking down the hill,
Then over the high railway bridge across
The winding Credit River, to find the lost trail.
Up the other side, a dark, thin pathway
By the old lime kiln, well grown over now
With vines and trees, over rocks, roots and stumps
To the base of the cliff, and looking up,
I wonder where the vultures are landing.
Still I stand there, quiet like another tree,
Still I stand there more and then, I hear it
Above on a shelf of rock—something moves.

I plot my course and climb the steep, rough face
Of the cliff, parallel to close tree trunks.
I can do this climb, I can reach that shelf,
And there, as I pull myself up, now there
I am face to face with the largest chick
Imaginable. Fluffy, white feathers,
Black beak, black beady eye, I am quite close.
Now his mouth gapes open with a great hiss
Like a baby dragon, enamouring
Me, tempting me to touch his feathered side.

But, now I feel a shadow on the wind.
I look up and there above is Mother,
Hovering close, real close, considering
What to do to me, wings spread full across—
An enormous presence, there to protect
Her young from me, a small interloper
Unwelcome on her bare piece of home rock,
Her aerie—and I, breathless with wonder
Gasp an apology and hope my feet
And hands can take me down safely because
Of course, I am alone there in Vulture
Land, having told no one my plan to go
Across the valley and up the cliff face.
One giant wing, the length and breadth of me,
Tips my way. One stroke of wing could take me
Tumbling down into those deep roots and rocks
And darkness like a vulture's dinner plate.

My apology holds, the vulture still
In the air, in graceful, forgiving mode,
Allows me my escape into the woods
Where she cannot follow for the dense trees.
I flee fast home again to where I now
Watch only, as the vultures drift upwards
And around on air currents and updrafts,
With new respect for modern dragons' lairs.

Merridy Cox-Bradley, *aside from creating poetry, is a technical writer and editor. She finds pleasure in the English language and the natural history of Ontario, where she lives. Follow Merridy on her blog, www.englishmanual.wordpress.com.*

Janine Georgiou-Zeck

ANGELS DRAPED IN RED AND WHITE

They took me in and kept me warm,
My rescuers from the darkest storm,
They shared their home, their food and hearts,
They showed me how forgiveness starts.

They lent a shoulder, a listening ear,
They warmed my chills and calmed my fears
Each one extended me a feather,
To build my wings and help me weather.

Countless patrons in this land,
Hearts that thrive on lending a hand.
Surely this is a step close to heaven,
Where the injured find a safe haven.

With new strong wings built with such love,
One wants to do well and rise above,
To show the kindhearted that all their care,
Was not a wasted affair.

A quilt of gifts from passersby
Has given me lift to help me fly,
My treasure of tears of thanks and joy;
So strong a storm cannot destroy.

It is with many thanks to you;
My life begins afresh and new,
My angels draped in red and white,
Thank you for my wings of flight.

CROW'S NEST

Sitting at the window,
On a cool September's eve,
In a quaint York Region bar,
Celebrating something achieved.

A small fragment of Britain,
Like a Tardis in a new place,
Temporary retreat from changes,
And a culturally different pace.

Specials!
Bangers Mash and Beans, Apple crumble, Cottage pie,
Liver and onions, Fish and chips,
Lots of flavours to try.

Plaid underfoot, royal velvet cushioned seat,
Heavy burgundy drapes, frame Newmarket's Prospect Street.

Culture shock in any new land,
Is the absolute norm,
But here we have such diversity,
And places to keep us warm.

To give us a glimpse of our previous home,
Without having to leave this space,
Allowing us the best of both worlds,
And a chance to embrace others.

A small paned-window setting,
With ducks swimming along the canal outside,
As the fall grasses begin to disappear,
Under the growing ice on the banks,
A reminder that this gem sits on Canadian soil.

I LOVE MY GARDEN

As much as I love what each season might bring,
While in winter my heart truly pines for the spring.

When it's crispy outside but a warm plus 5,
Into my boots and coat I will dive.
It's above 4 degrees and I'm loving this day,
Because months of minus something,
Took my garden away.

I rake and I sweep, rearranging the yard,
While no bugs, rain or snow are making it hard,
The gardens are cleaner with each melting day,
As the ice disappears, where the plants will lay.

Sitting by the window,
Where the sun beams strong,
Are my tiny saplings,
Growing all April long.

When the last frost is gone,
It's time to invest,
In the soil, plants and food,
To bring out the best.

With tips from neighbours, and help from friends,
My little green thumbs get thicker stems.

There's a magic in the garden,
That extends beyond the cold,
That connects us with our land,
And unites us young and old.

ISABELLA ISLAND

Awakening to the sound of the loon on the lake,
I grab my blanket, step outside and watch the morning break.
The boat gently nudges the dock, as I look across the bay.
Fresh light sparkles on soft movement;
And life arises for the day.

As the gentle morning mist clears from view.
Bass leap for bugs in the distance and fishing calls.
But it is time to relax and take it all in,
With the warm scent of coffee,
And the woodpecker chiseling at the pine.

The family starts to stir, joining me one by one,
The delicious scent of breakfast fills the air,
As we warm with the sun.

The day is inviting; it's time for a swim,
Leave it all behind and jump in!
Clear through to the bottom, plants tickle our feet,
Creatures weave in and out of the grasses,
Looking for food to eat.

Turtles, snakes and frogs, greet us at the dock,
Sometimes in the boat, which gives us a bit of a shock!
Boating across the water, spray soaks us, soon to dry,
A deer swims to the shore, as birds of prey pass us by.

Tie off at Rose Point Marina, and head to Parry Sound,
To enjoy a couple of hours of shopping and looking around.

The fish are biting, no rain for days,
The sun gently sets in an array of colours,
As the water settles and the crickets serenade.

As daylight sinks down behind the trees,
The islands become silhouettes against an abundance of stars.
Quaint shimmers of light reflect off the water,
As slowing waves lap against the rocks.

Back to our Island oasis, we get the fire pit stoked,
Grab blankets to huddle up in and enjoy some trout that's smoked.

Summer escape soon becomes fall vibrancy, and time to leave
Memories of Georgian Bay
Will echo in our hearts,
Making the coming winter a little warmer.

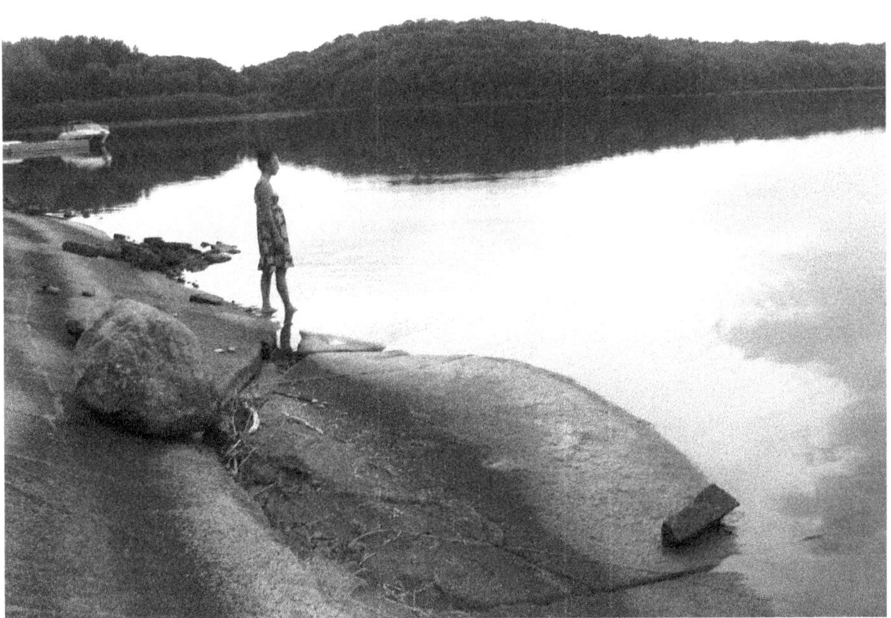

By the Lake by Janine Georgiou-Zeck

NOT FORGOTTEN

Their spirits were tested,
Far more than life intended,
They fought for our freedom,
Survived things we can't imagine.

They were obedient visionaries,
Sacrificing their natural path,
So that those they could not see,
Would have peace.

Leaving behind a beautiful start,
A family, friends,
Adapting to tumultuous times,
To ensure that war ends.

These are the angels on which we rest our heads,
When we sleep safely in our beds.

These are the pavers of roads,
On which we have safe passage,
The gatekeepers who set us free,
Never shall I take for granted,
All that was passed on to me.

Our Canadian soldiers,
Who fought for all we know,
You are not forgotten,
As we flourish and grow.

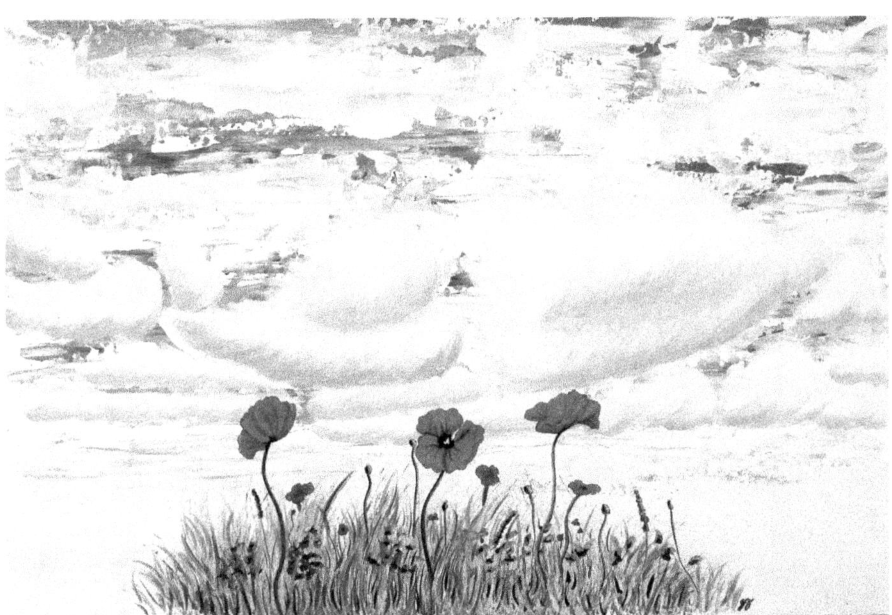

Red Poppies by Janine Georgiou-Zeck

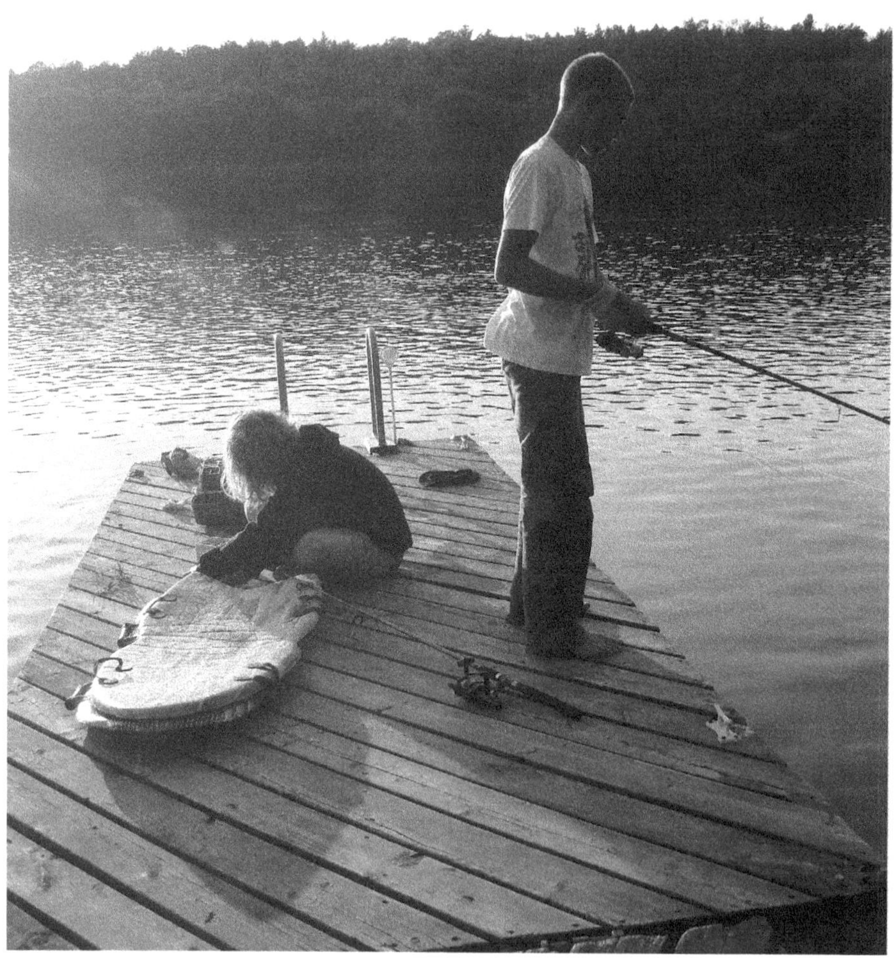

Josephine and Jacob fishing on the pier by Janine Georgiou-Zeck

WHERE DO I BELONG?

Where the snow gently drifts past the windows at night,
And looks like icing at first morning light.

Where the days slowly warm until the ground is thawed,
So the vibrant spring colours can be adored.

Where summer days are long, kissed with tropical heat,
Sounds of children joyfully splash along the beach,

Where leaves transform into a rainbow of colours,
As the crisp fall air meets them.

Where the wilderness invites us,
And overwhelms our hearts with its' vast beauty.

Where we join others from all around the world,
As they visit attractions or find a home.

Where the smell of cinnamon buns fills the malls,
Or Tim Horton's coffee calls.

Where local Maple syrup,
Pours gently over blueberry pancakes.
And cottages overlook,
The Great Lakes.

This is where I belong.

YOURS AND MINE

You are young,
But you have experienced much,
You are strong and determined,
But not out of touch.

At times you have such heights,
And at others, you're low,
To celebrate achievements,
And honour those you know.

You are crisp and bright,
With a meaningful design,
You represent a history,
That is yours and mine.

You have only one vibrant colour,
Yet you represent a rainbow,
Your background is plain,
Yet we bask in its' glow.

Your corners curve and flap in the breeze,
Back and forth you sway,
Shifting gently,
On this lightly windy day.

You look over on what you're proud of,
Like an angel in flight.
You stand for us, as we stand for you,
Our flag of red and white.

LAND OF GIANTS

This airport – a portal to what I don't know.
One step out the door and away I go,
In a cab on a fairytale winter's eve,
In awe of the space and the air I can breathe.

Fresh is this Land of Giants,
Wonders new and fascinating,
Life – a slowly unwrapping gift.

Gazing at the road ahead,
It seems to never end,
Like a passageway for Giants to tread.

Snow and ice shimmer on rooftops and trees,
There's a sweet smell on the breeze,
Where will this road take me?

Possibility – the door has opened,
My journey has really begun,
I'm ready Giants,
Let's have some fun!

CHASING THE MONARCH[1]

Fluttering about,
Landing on distant flowers,
A splendid monarch glides towards us,
A flash of vermillion.

Giggling my little one rises,
Jumping up and down,
Running softly through the grass,
Towards the vibrant spark.

"Look," he yells,
"It landed." He points at a rose.
Bold orange contrasts against the white petals.
He moves in closer.

Opening and closing its wings gently,
Strong black lines,
And small white specks
Closer still, we see the creature drink.

Up it flies again,
As the little hand goes to gently touch,
Then the chase once again across the grass
Pleading "Come back butterfly."

---

1 Monarch butterflies are easily recognized for their striking colours, black, orange and white. The curious thing about the North American monarchs is their late summer, early fall migration to the United States and Mexico from as far north as Canada.

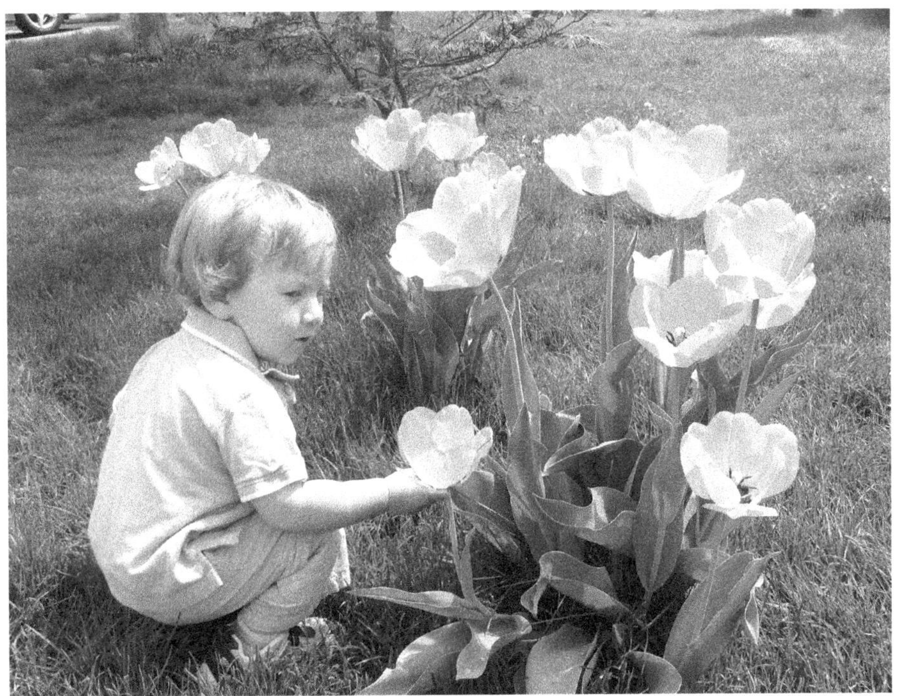

Jasper Chasing Butterflies by Janine Georgiou-Zeck

OUR OASIS

Two-level home,
Cookie cutter in style,
White siding, red brick,
Grey patio tile.

Detached Newmarket home, built in 'seventy three,
Not a palace or flashy, but just right for me.

Open concept main level,
With cottage-like charm,
Enough space for the children,
Enough room for some calm.

A studio area, where art classes are taught,
Creativity blossoms that can't be bought.

A deck,
With direct heat from the sun,
Where I can relax,
And the children have fun.

On a warm summer's eve,
When the nets are drawn,
We have shelter from bugs,
Or a gentle rain storm.

Yes it's ordinary,
Compared to some places,
But to my family,
It is our very own 'Canadian Oasis.'

Janine Georgiou-Zeck *is an Artist Educator, who lives in York Region. She is an Artist-in-Residence for the York Region District School Board. She is a mother of three, who loves creating educational material for books and integrated workshops. Janine established Janine's Art School and www.jzartstudio.wix.com in 2006 and has been teaching art on these forums and in York Region schools for ten years. Poetry is close to her heart as a way of channeling joy, appreciation and the everyday.*

Ed Woods

TTC REPLICA

my friend of youthful times
had a backyard project
to exact a streetcar
of Toronto Transit

driver controls
fare box to wheels
rooftop power pole
seats and leather handgrips
but due to logistics he settled
on a precise plywood shell

my sturdy bicycle
carried home heavy items
from the maintenance depot
how the seats arrived
is still a mystery

years later as a transport driver
I delivered railway track
to the same yard
and commented on his project

a mechanic was summoned
and was laughingly relieved
to verify he had not lost his mind
when for two years so many parts
disappeared off his repair bench
during a lunch break

PAYROLL

service call done
banking unit fixed
I fly my aircraft northbound
Along the coastal Rockies
a sudden storm blocks landing
a local statement hits true
that British Columbia clouds
are billowy bright and beautiful
but are hard at the centers

lightning makes flight instruments
point to a false north
whatever was on my mind
quickly bumped to second place
by desire of asphalt safety
over oceanic impact

controllers allow a path
behind a swaying jet
above sequenced strobes
to white hot runway lights

the buffeted jet crew
cool under fire
place a radio request
for a good fishing spot
as they have three days off

I feel they must be from
a hurricane or tornado zone

at home a hot shower
flows stress down the drain
in a few days my payroll
will reflect this service call
devoid of the extraneous effort

MILESTONES

young men left their farms
bursting with war effort pride
to show the enemy
a bit of Canadian rural justice

a quick war with no losses
then home to celebration

but the human toll
touched all nations
on the ground
and in the sky

the horror deep-embedded
lasted long after armistice
heavy tears continue to fall
in many a beer mug
or wineglass
continues to saturate many a pillow

photos from those days
bring pause in the daily round
X'd out of the military
some from natural causes

post war success
health and possessions
country drives to picnic
in every home
the best of technology

today the war-aged
enjoy youthful liberties

fruition of my effort
roosted a milestone
as in today's mail
arrived the first
veteran's cheque

FREEDOM[1]

it's time to bring in the harvest
waves of corn stalks sway
in the winds of freedom
I clutch corn in my hands – my corn
grown on fertile land – my land
a glorious cash crop – my cash

two years have passed
from the sounds of terror

of rattling chains
pulse drumming
to the crack of vicious whips
reminders never to heal

fear-filled moonlighting in swamps
a plan of escape from the South
afraid the boss-man would swoop and kill
if snakes and alligators miss their chance

images of a boxcar on steel rails
travelling through deep thicket trails
never the same route twice
a worn pathway, a risk to avoid

thousand miles of fearful steps
breathing misty night air
every heartbeat pounded in my ears
salt tearing my eyes
sometimes crying for relief from the blur
sometimes crying for relief from slavery
crouching at the least strange sound
a twig breaking brought panic
a meow became a lion's roar

life entrusted to strangers
of a different colour
celebrating right to freedom
left to the last whistle stop
at Upper Canada

a place where I can now own land
and forever not be owned
the property mine to farm
for *my* benefit
cash in *my* hands
for *my* keepsake
earned and banked
for *myself*

to help fund the next safe haven
along the underground railroad

1 This poem is based on the 'freedom' sought by slaves escaping slavery in the South in the 1800s. These slaves moved northwards to free states or to Canada via the underground railroad, which was in fact a network of secret routes and safe houses. It is estimated that over 30,000 slaves used the underground railroad to escape to various points across the Canadian border from Nova Scotia across to British Columbia. Many entered through southwestern Ontario (particularly Windsor and Chatham). Courtesy Historica Canada www.blackhistorycanada.ca

FULL MOON FLIGHT

I lift off Vancouver's runway
over blackened ocean
into sacred night
gentle as a swaddled newborn
is lifted from a cradle
in mother's celebration

aircraft drawn towards full moon
reaches cruise altitude
parallels the Rockies southbound
my rugged companions
haloed guidance
glistening snowcaps drift by
enchantingly

clouds gather
friendly for now
in stationary stance
as if in awe of moon glow

prominent peaks highlighted
like a string of beacons
assists high altitude adventurers
of nighttime travel

moonlight tracks across the ocean
illuminate surf waves
on slopes rising to black sky
valley clouds form a cotton ball blanket
lit crimson from towns below

again our planet reveals
its marvels, its beauty
in the wonders
of our earthly travel

NEW IMMIGRANT

great excitement
as this jet is cleared
for an approach to land

hopes of a new start
in a new land
disembarking to high altitude air
charged pure and clean

pounding heartbeat
anxious in anticipation
of all this land has to offer

this is my first adventure anywhere
since letting go of mother's hand
away from father's scrutiny

will I be successful
or shocked to the core
and retreat on the next
available flight home

exiting the terminal
a protesting crowd
inconsiderate and cruel
feels I don't deserve
the right to enter this land
they jeer a newcomer
seeking fortune and glory

am I no different than you
in mutual betterment of society
contributing to this land
to enhance the economy?

working my way out to a taxicab
I cannot fathom why
protesters in Calgary
changed so drastically
from offering 'White Hat' hospitality
to sending me back
from where I came
to freeze in the dark
of Toronto

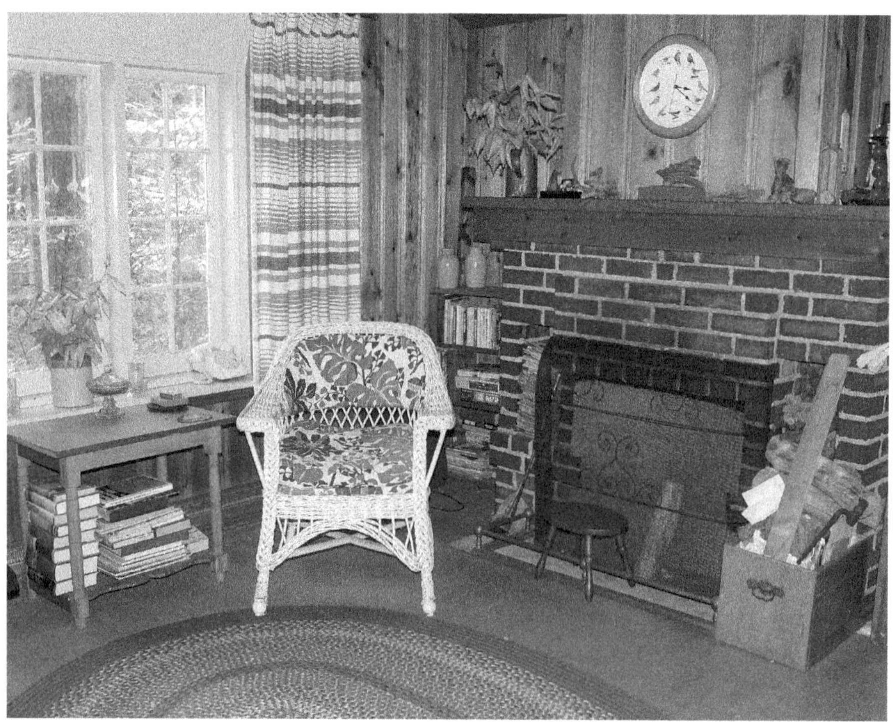

Cabin by Merridy Cox-Bradley

A SPIRITED VISIT

I was the on-call service technician at my company's branch in Edmonton, Alberta, when a call came in from the only bank in Spirit River. The call was put through to me as I am able to fly our company aircraft to the town's airport, which is adjacent to the highway and hence arrive the same day. Once landed, I loaded the tool cases and a parts box onto a specialized dolly cart, which I had constructed myself for such occasions, and began to walk towards town under a brilliant blue sky.

I crossed the highway, then over multiple railway tracks and through grain elevators to a sidewalk. As I walked towards the bank, I spied many people peeking at me through storefront windows, obviously wondering about the stranger in town. I waved and nodded to them in succession, then entered the bank that was a beehive of activity with staff on the phones and many customers.

I requested access to the vault where the problem was supposed to be according to the service call, but then the manager walked over to ask for I.D. I produced my company card. He asked why I wanted to go into the vault. I said it was for a service call on a machine. As an attempt at humour, I said if he preferred the machine could be repaired at the counter and then tested with real money once it was back in the vault. The humour was lost on him. He asked if my car was working fine or did it break down on the highway. I replied I own a van and it is working fine. He asked where I had parked it. I replied "in Edmonton." He asked how I got here. I explained that his town has an airport so I flew our company aircraft over. He turned to the staff and explained my arrival. Then some of the staff members immediately phoned their town-mates. Apparently their peek-a-boo neighbors had called to advise bank staff to watch out for a guy coming down the street with boxes on a dolly cart! He may be there to rob the bank!

I told the manager that should this scenario be true, then I had obviously not thought the plan through very well, with only one highway through this remote area and a dolly cart as a getaway vehicle and no hiding of my identity. How far did they think I would get on foot with no food or water when the nearest town is 80 miles away, which is why I flew here in the first place to save long hours of driving.

The manager joined me outside where I pointed to the white and orange aircraft visible across the highway. To ease his embarrassment, I offered to take him for a ride after the repair work. He led me into the vault where repairs were completed. I asked if anyone wanted a ride before my flight back home, but everyone, including customers, declined. I told them to come outside in about thirty minutes to see an air show and that when I pass by the town and rock the wings then that would be my signal for departure.

I lifted off the runway towards the main street lined with people waiting to watch my ten-minute illegal mini-air show and on my last pass, I picked up speed and climbed steeply. This concluded my service call to Spirit River.

Ed Woods *was born in Toronto and now lives in Dundas, Ontario. Through workshops with established writers he received encouragement to expand upon life experiences through poetry. His topics range from the serious to comedic, with observations or insight written from the heart. A favorite topic is aviation, delivered from the pilot's point of view through the limitless panorama of a wrap-around windshield.*

Silvana Sangiuliano

AMONG THE MAGNOLIA TREES

walking miles in a seemingly endless day
on rugged mountainous terrain
trail barely wide enough
for tiny wavering feet
women steadily balance baskets
on heads, hauling laundry

kneeling on stones by undulating river
weary hands scrub vigorously on jagged rocks
agitating, wringing, washing immaculate sheets

kapok, laurel, and magnolia trees
dot the lush landscape
beneath canopy of rainforest
shade beckons below branches of understory
devoid of sunlight

calm and beauty juxtaposed with hardship
mask an arduous existence at best
lines of pain and sacrifice
etched upon their faces
like folds in sheets rubbed
between raw fingers

oppression lingers
in dispirited hearts
desire to leave for new country
assimilate into cultural mosaic
with those who went before them
to a land filled with hope and promise
Canada

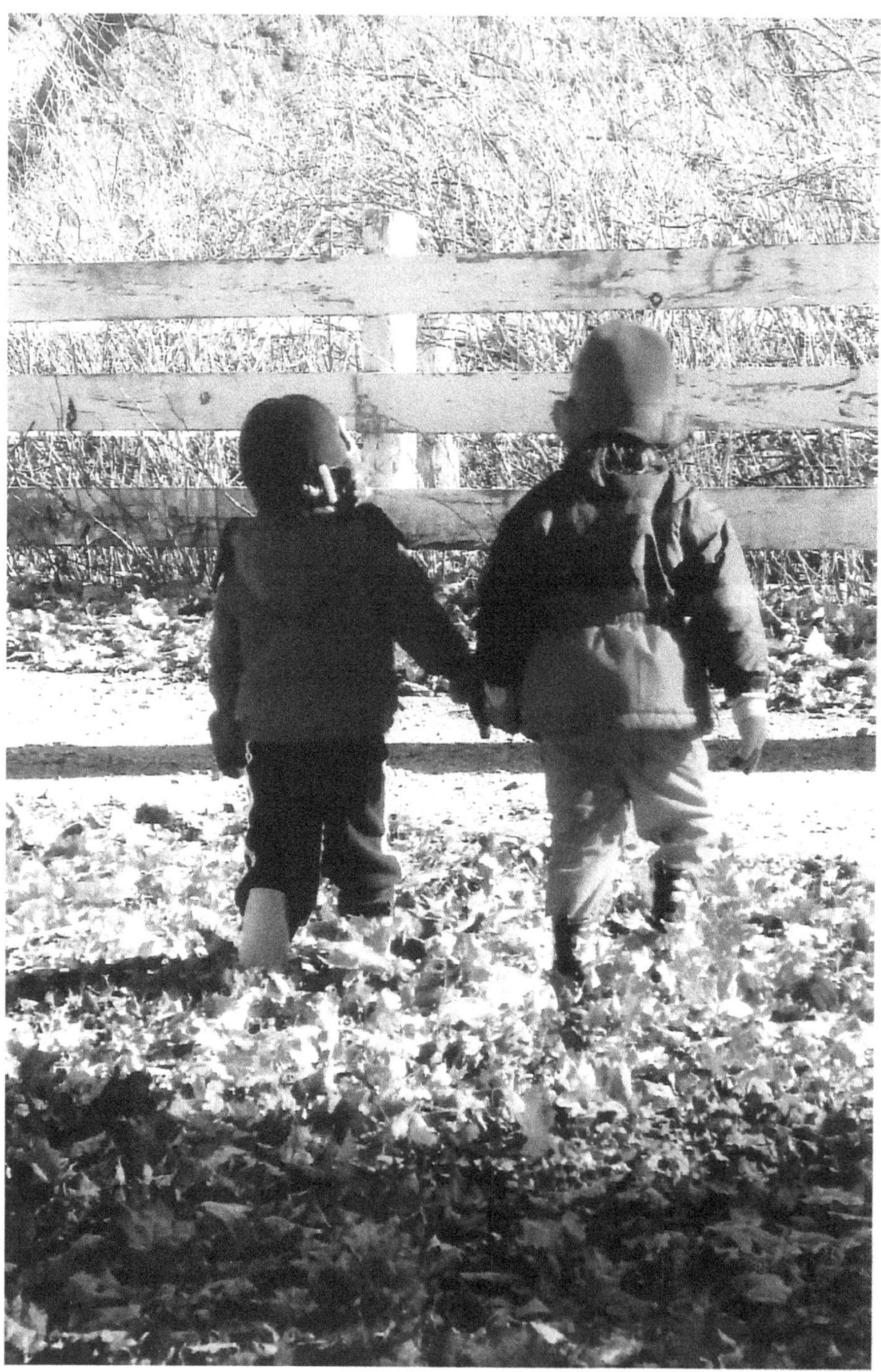

Silvana Sangiuliano's sons Joshua and Jonah in Maple Park.

MAPLE PARK

two small brothers bewildered in thought
pass swings, slides, and climbing bars
curious feet in yellow and navy blue rain boots
crunch through frostbitten leaves
kicking up fall colours
beneath overhang of majestic maple trees
in a characteristic Ontario landscape

shadows of a three-foot child
the other just inches taller
follow their inquisitive path

pint-sized geniuses exploring nature
look up at an Osprey's nest
on their way to search for a beaver dam

tiny bodies
dive beneath weather worn fence
squirm leaving muddy imprints
reinforced posts hold windswept boards
faded from years of shielding passers-by from the lake

an aluminum fishing boat
tethered with a bowline knot to a floating wooden dock
bobs gently
little boys jump up and down
enjoying dizzying movement of the platform
before they are called to go home

CONCERTO IN THE COUNTRY

night befalls, tranquil wind whispers
Canadian flag waves softly in the breeze
maple leaves sway in pianissimo movement
tinkling silver chimes ring softly

friends nestle upon Adirondack chairs
encircling a crackling fire in the Ontario countryside
roasting trillium white marshmallows
listening to emerald cedar burning
disintegrating like sparklers
hissing and dissipating on a festive evening
whistling fireworks explode
kaleidoscopic streaks reach toward the Milky Way
painted across silence of darkness
echoing in ambient light

whole-hearted laughter emanates in a crescendo
in unison with the popping of an impermeable cork
crystal glasses clink to a boisterous "Cheers!"

nocturnal male crickets chirp an operetta
in pursuit of the female
their music rivals with June bugs
buzzing and swarming in the blackness

spontaneous sky starts to sprinkle rain
dripping happily, uninhibited
an Italian Tarantella it dances
pinging against the metal eavestrough
staccato ringing in the wetness
arms thrown toward the shadowy skies
spinning, skipping, surrendering
a pirouette to nature's impromptu music
raindrops permeate our being
mystical acoustics awaken the soul

SAVOURED MEMORIES

in the sanctuary of the kitchen
a haven for family gatherings
background of soothing opera
Pavarotti's aria *Nessun Dorma*
penetrates the tranquil Sunday morning
legato ties together ancestral bond

outside the window overlooking the balcony
resting dew drops awaken, finding their place on the grass
mourning doves nest in the cherry tree
clothes drape freely on the line, strung between pear trees
swaying in the breeze
whispering myths
muted by the artful folding of immaculate sheets
holding corners in each hand
pulling taut
snapping in the current
crisp as the dawn of a new day

daybreak would see the collecting of
bright green variegated zucchini
adorned with blossoms, hue of an egg yolk
cracked to make fritters

ruby red fruit nurtured by Papà in the garden
boiled, peeled, and canned, sealing flavours
jars stored through winter in the cold cellar
in the company of salami and prosciutto
hanging from butcher's string neatly tied to rafters

sauce simmering
smell of sweet ripened tomatoes
scents of oregano and basil emanate from the pot
stimulating nostalgia
wooden spoon stained with years
of family tradition and folklore

stirring secrets and untold legends
Mamma presses against the countertop
kneading, rolling dough, precisely cutting homemade fettuccine
sifted flour speckles upon her apron

aroma of Italian cuisine permeates the country air
loved ones sit at the oversized wooden picnic table
draped with a freshly pressed red and white checkered cloth
the colours of the Canadian flag
uniting generations of family
a joyous cornerstone of their lives

beneath the cloudless sky
glistening summer sun dances on crystal glasses
clinking "Salute!" "Cheers!"
reflecting laughter and joy
swirling, sipping red wine
made with proud hands
siphoned from wicker encased demijohns

antipasto of marinated artichoke hearts,
dried black olives, tomatoes kissed by the sun, and
savoury cured meats alongside provolone and Asiago cheese
satiate salivating palates

colander drains strands of al dente glory
pasta twirls on plates
sucked into mouths, filling souls

emerald green rapini marry with garlic
tomatoes bathe in olive oil
Calabrese bread dips
absorbing richness of flavour
tingling pink velvet tongues

an espresso soothes spirits
excited chatter against a backdrop of serenity
stalks of golden wheat gently sway in the field
undulating like the sea

meandering along a path forged through the bush
white trilliums, the flower emblem of Ontario
scatter throughout the woodland floor
in the nearby meadow
picking dandelions
downy florets blow, petite parachutes
feathers soaring in the wind

pastures laden with buttercups
chins bathed in yellow glow
crab apple and purple plum trees rise above
the majestic garden overflowing with
magenta sunset swiss chard, green beans,
maroon radicchio, cucumbers, corn, and chives
emerging through the rich soil blanketing the landscape
carefree tomato vines intertwine
woven like the tapestry of life

preparing our bountiful harvest
sharing stories on the veranda
Mamma's azure eyes sparkle like the Ionian Sea
Papà's chestnut eyes smile
strength reminiscent of mountainous terrain
horizon streaked with violet and burnt orange
as the sun sets before us in a sapphire sky
welcoming us into the night

Mamma says the moon follows us wherever we go
basking in wonderment beneath its glow
telling twilight folk tales
in front of flickering flames of fire

as embers begin to wane
we return to the sanctuary of the kitchen
immersed in smells lingering within
savoured memories
permeate the core of our existence

STOLEN INNOCENCE

transparent virgin skin stretched
over quail-like bones
calloused hands depict courage
in dark, putrid factories
tiny distressed fingers work feverishly to produce
designer apparel to adorn an affluent world
petite bodies tunnel through perilous mines
labouring in deadly, noxious environments
for diamonds to bejewel fleshy, wealthy fingers

corporate obfuscation of conglomerate exploitation
gluttons satisfy hunger and greed
while malnourished, impoverished hearts
of bread-winners of the family
find piece work barely enough for food
destitution and hardship feed prosperity
consumerism and materialism dominate lives
in a vicious circle where
bystanders are mere passive enablers

peer beyond hollows in sallow faces
see through windows into empty souls
witness the robbing of childhood, dispossessing of tutelage
drug trafficking, pornography, slavery, prostitution
stripping away formative years

eyes stare into the abyss
in an imaginary looking glass
a portal to freedom reveals itself
escape to Canada
beautiful, embracing land where
children play, read, breathe freely,
laugh wholeheartedly, without inhibition
never growing old before their time

PAPÀ, STOP THE CAR!

"Papà, stop the car!" The ribbed sheet metal we are riding on shifts left to right on icy road patches. My father can't hear me over the deafening vrooming sound of the thumping, thundering engine, despite the fact he is sticking his head out the car window looking back at us. The whipping wind whooshes fiercely in his face. His curly brown hair catches snowflakes, as he swiftly switches gears on the car's standard transmission.

My sister Loredana and brothers Frank and Greg scream with joy as we ride on our homemade sled, hitched with a rusty chain to Papà's 1970 red Fiat 124. This boxy Italian import holds its own as the 76 horsepower engine tugs us banging and bouncing behind down the 7th line of Beeton. Snow clogs the alternating grooves of our impromptu sled. A chill whips through our throbbing bones. Our eyes squint through veils of blowing snow. Chapped lips snap shut trying to avoid inhaling the car's exhaust fumes. Nose hair begins to freeze. Wiggling our nostrils to dislodge the frost, we hold on tight, swerving around corners, listening to the clanging and banging of the chain. I hope the lengthy links don't come apart, sending us into the deep ditch. Quivering fingers turn numb from clasping. Unexpectedly, the Fiat comes to a screeching stop.

"Aw, is it over already?" Greg, the youngest, asks.

"That's it for today kids. I have to get some work done."

"I was just getting into it," Loredana wails.

"Hey you guys, let's go on a snowmobile ride!" Frank says.

We jump on our navy blue '79 Kawasaki 440 Invader snowmobiles. Zigzagging through the freshly fallen snow, beneath the skis, we feel every bump over remnants of cornstalks planted earlier that year. The wind blasts into our faces. Snow crystalizes on our lashes as we careen through the open field.

"Yahoo!" we yell, racing through the countryside. One hand grips the throttle, feeding fuel to the engine, the other gives a thumbs-up. Weaving through the bush, we imprint tracks between coniferous and deciduous trees. Unsuspecting majestic maples, pines, spruce, and oak stand still in winter's breeze. Shielded beneath the white winter blanket, acorns, pinecones, evergreen needles, and trilliums are asleep. Deer scurry at the sound of roaring engines and boisterous voices.

As we veer through the fields, Mamma stands on the balcony shivering in her apron motioning us with her hand to come in for dinner, "*Venite a mangiare.*"

Easing off the throttle, we begin to slow down, finally coming to a halt. Leaping off our snowmobiles, we dive into four-foot snowdrifts, rolling and rolling around. Powdery flakes fall softly upon chilled cheeks. We raise and lower our arms and legs becoming one with the swirling snow. Listening to the scrunching of our snowsuits rubbing against the snowy surface, we leave impressions of angels. Running back to the house with excitement, we snap off icicles where heat meets intense cold.

Together with Papà, we gather some wood, cut earlier in the year and neatly stacked in a corner of the veranda, in preparation for blustery wintry days like this.

"Let's go inside," Papà says.

"I'm soaked!" cries Loredana.

We peel off layers of winter clothing and hang them in every available spot to dry.

"Mamma, we had so much fun!" Greg calls out.

"I hope you're hungry."

"It smells good in here," Frank says.

The aroma of homemade Calabrese bread and minestrone soup fills the air. Mamma says, "This is one of my favourite dishes. I used to eat this all the time when I was growing up in Italy." She licks the spoon to taste. "Mmm…"

I take a few steps towards the kitchen, "I'll get the bowls."

In the living room, kindling begins to crackle. The smell of wood burning permeates the country air. A roaring fire warms our home.

I am forever enchanted by Canadian winters and such happy family memories. The '70s would see so much snow, unlike today. We would bury ourselves indoors for days, peering at drifts from within. In front of the hearth, we would watch the snow fall, gently descending in its untouched splendour. Sparkling diamonds, crystal prisms beckoned interaction. I long for those winters where snow was plentiful and was the backdrop for our rural adventures.

Outside, I can still hear Papà revving the engine of that little red Fiat.

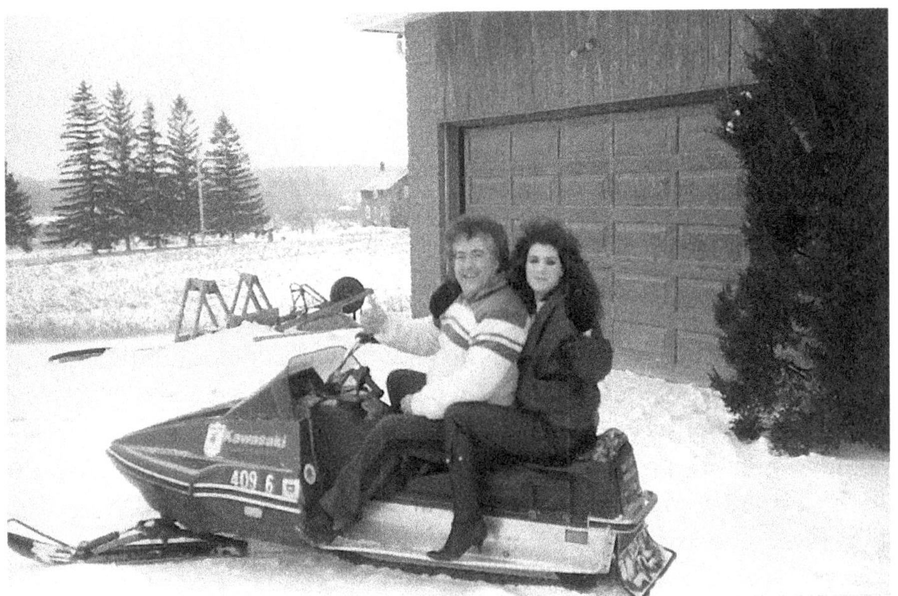

Silvana Sangiuliano with her father on the Kawasaki snowmobile in later years.

MY SCHOOL DAYS

The yellow Blue Bird school bus barrels down the gravel road, leaving a trail of dust in its wake, just outside of Beeton. We feel every bump on the 7th Line, like craters on the moon. We fly down the steep and treacherous 'Murder Hill,' coined for its infamous black ice.

Arriving at Bradford High, the majestic maple leaf banner, flying in red and white splendour from the flagpole, welcomes us. We race to our lockers before the start of the Canadian National Anthem. If we are late and caught in the halls on our way to homeroom, we know Mr. Lindsay will give us detention. We stand still, listening to the patriotic words coming through the loudspeakers, "O Canada, we stand on guard for thee." Then, off to class we go, with the detention pink slip in hand.

We sit at our wooden desks, which have hardened chewing gum stuck underneath. Using pens stored in the inkwell, we scribble graffiti depicting our favourite rock bands on foolscap paper or in our notebooks, forgetting about the lessons. Quickly, we hide our drawings inside the storage compartment of our desk as the teacher walks by, careful not to snap the desk lid shut on our fingers. The cold metal bar joining the desk to my seat, nudges my hip as I lean over, secretly passing notes to my sister Loredana and friend Sarah.

During science class, Mr. Buchanan, who has a striking resemblance to Einstein, dashes in, tails of his lab coat flap in the breeze. He boasts the dishevelled look of a genius, happy and eager to have us watch things bubble and blow up, while testing hypotheses.

The science lab is not the only place where ingredients simmer and stew. The kitchen setting in home economics class is quite eventful, especially when we start throwing flour at one another behind the teacher's back.

If I wasn't in the science lab or the kitchen, you would probably find me dancing to a disco beat on the gymnasium stage beneath the imaginary mirror ball.

Gymnastics and Track and Field were part of my school years. Whether I got rope burn from climbing thick, twisted sisal ropes suspended from rafters, did dizzying cartwheels on the balancing beam, jumped off the springboard over the vaulting horse, or competed in running, high jump, and long jump, my stamina and endurance were tested.

A different kind of drill occurs in my Business Communications class. I can still hear the clickity-clack of the Olivetti-Underwood typewriter keys. My typing teacher Mrs. Boultbee's stern voice resonates in my mind, "Accuracy not speed. Don't look down at the keys. Keep your back straight. Eyes forward."

As my shorthand teacher Mrs. Bennington dictates, I frantically write symbols and abbreviations turning the pages trying to keep up with her. I later develop a bump on my finger from tightly gripping my pencil, as I nervously scribble short form in my stenography book between the red ruled lines. All that hard work would see me place second in the finals in the Ontario shorthand competition.

We spend our lunch either in the cafeteria avoiding food fights, or take a walk towards downtown along the gravel shoulder to the Chat 'n' Chew restaurant. We put coins in the jukebox and listen to rock tunes. Loredana, Sarah, and I split gravy-drenched fries and a sticky honey bun three-ways. Then, we play arcade games before heading back to school.

After school, as we stepped off the bus, our mother, waiting at the end of the driveway, always greeted us with hugs.

I often look back and wonder where my teachers are today. As I write this, lost in pleasant memories, I can only hope that in some small way, I am paying homage to the teachers who helped shape my life and encouraged me to be all that I am. For to this day, I carry their words of wisdom within my heart. I can still visualize their faces. I can hear their voices. The laughter of students and the sound of the bell ringing, echo in my mind.

I can still see the majestic Canadian flag flying high in its glory over the untouched tree-lined fields. I swallow hard as a lump forms in my throat. My eyes well up, thinking how quickly the years have passed since I bid farewell to my old school.

Looking back on that yellow Blue Bird school bus, I see a trail of dust in its wake, just off that country road in Bradford.

Silvana Sangiuliano *was born in Toronto to Italian immigrant parents who settled in the countryside near Beeton. A writer, editor, and teacher, she has an English degree from the University of Guelph, is an accredited English teacher through the University of Cambridge, England, and studied at the Italian Cultural Institute. Silvana's poetry and prose has appeared in several publications and has won and been shortlisted in literary contests.*

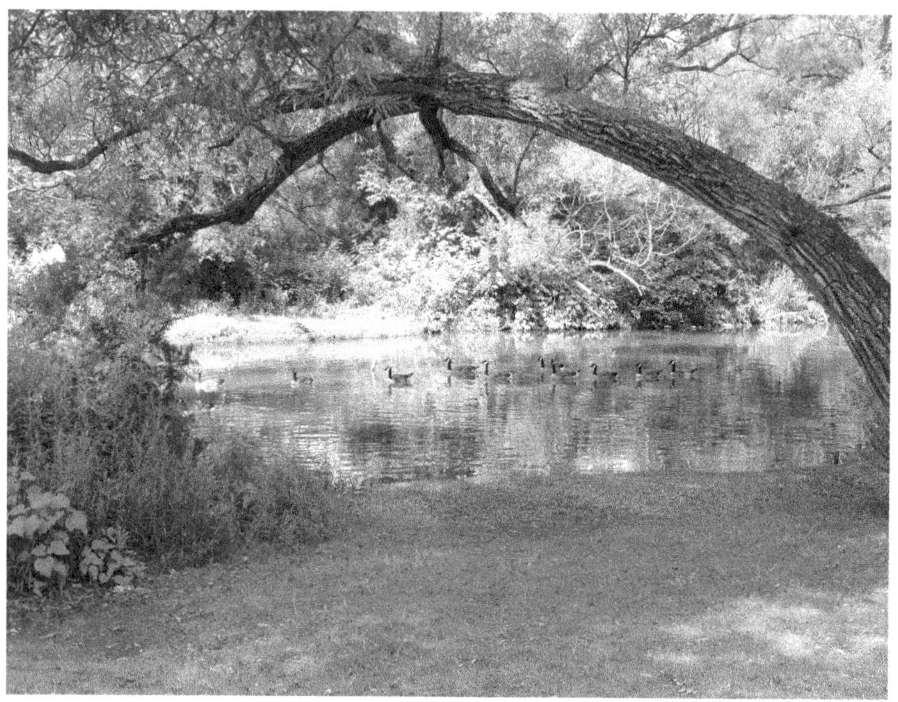

Photograph by Janine Georgiou-Zeck

Lindsay W. Albert

SEASONS

Summer

Daylight lingers
into late evening

Gardens abound
with an array of colours

Beaches warmed
by sun's radiant heat

School's out
children at play

Autumn

Daylight dwindles
colourful flowers fade

Trees transform
into vivid hues

Animals scurry
winter stores to prepare

Breezes blow
bringing cooler air

Winter

Tree skeletons
stand stark in the cold

Coniferous trees
hold on to their green

Snowy blanket
insulates the earth

Freezing air
nips at the flesh

Spring

Rain showers
nourish vast flora

New growth
rises through soil

Young emerge
from dens and nests

Life revived
from what appeared dead

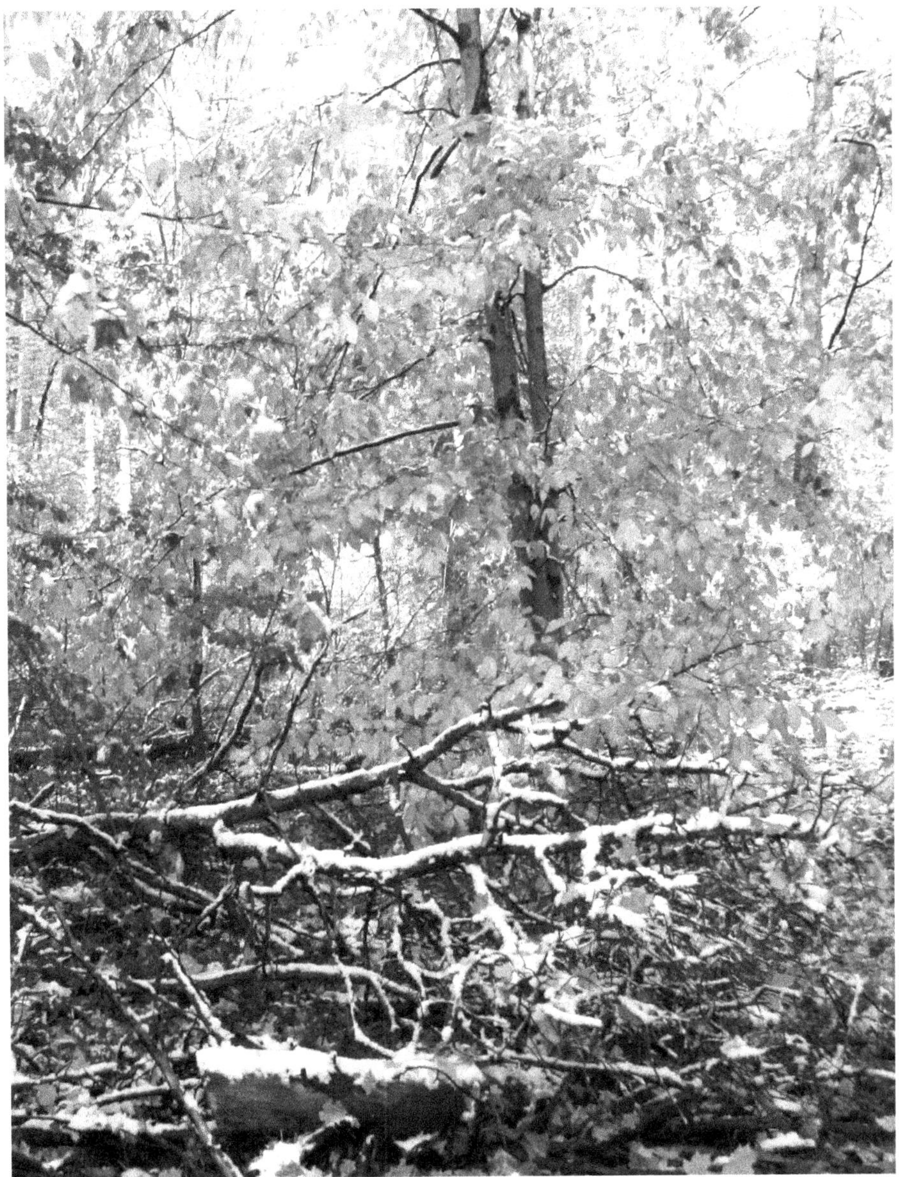

Early Snow by Nadia Tretikov

FREE TO BE ME

All I ever wanted
was to be free to be me

Not to have to conform
to what others say I should be

My strengths to be nurtured
to bring out the best in me

Don't condemn my weakness
for no good will this serve me

For inside my weakness
lies strength yet undiscovered

Accept all that I am
what is liked and what it is not

For I'm a whole person
not something to tear apart

Unconditional love
I seek to give and receive

With love and acceptance
I can live free to be me

GOOSE FOR A NATION

Characteristic
black and white markings
Each in their sameness
distinctly unique
Soul mates forever
till death befalls one
Nurture their offspring
to jointly provide
safety, food, shelter,
life skills to survive.
Flock community
watch o'er each other
calling out warnings
when danger is nigh
Fly V-formation
one taking the lead
Not ego driven
knows when to fall back
to rest and to glide
Entrusting the next
to listen and lead
as all contribute
to their common goal
Our Canada Goose
flying strong and free
has earned its rank as
Canada's icon

Lindsay W. Albert, *born and raised in Canada, developed a love for books and reading in her preschool years. At age 7, she began to write stories and poems as a source of healing expression. In recent years, she has been reading her poems at various poetry events in the GTA. Her poems have been published in three anthologies:* The Courtneypark Connection *(2013),* The Labour of Love *(2013) and* The Literary Connection, Volume 1 *(2014). Lindsay is currently working on her memoire and a collection of her poems on the subject of grief and loss.*

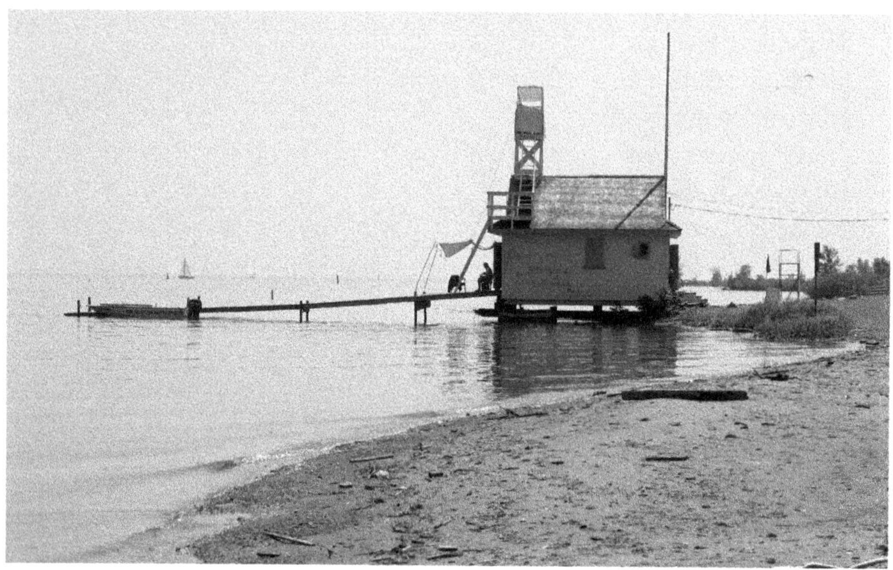

Lifeguard House Lake Ontario by Nina Munteanu

Josie Di Sciascio-Andrews

SUNRISE OVER LAKE ONTARIO

white seagulls perch
on grey driftwood
on beaches of sand and stones
early in the morning
when the orange sun
rises majestic over Lake Ontario
hugging the planet with fire
blowing light
across blue waves
filling my eyes with happiness

welcome gift
this vermilion warmth
I seek all year

this summer gladness
that takes me back
to all the sunrises of my life
before heartbreak
before the fall in darkened skies
when scenes like this were enough

my heart in a diorama
the earth's colours and mine
one

SUMMER DREAMS

Oakville pier
disappears in fog
on hot, muggy mornings
lake and sky blending in grey mist

on the wharf
the lighthouse beckons the eye
red stripe on white
beyond mounds of wild grass
blue chicory
silver lace

along the Sixteenth Mile's murky waters
sailboats' tall masts sway
hypnotic

Scarab, Dreaming, Ulysses

names for adventure
hulls to sail away on
at high seas

away from torpid waters
into blue oceans
new worlds
the sun

OF LOVE AND WRITING

you cannot force the poem
it comes when it will
on butterfly wings of kismet

sails whole with wind
blowing along deep blue oceans
hide their reasoned intricacies
beneath reality's perfect skin

words too, they pull
mind, heart, senses
to shared images of worlds
we all have known

like the dark, green brush strokes
of weather-bent pines
cutting against wisps of white
in cool blue, northern skies

the evenings spent casting lines
in ponds of golden sunsets
while longings took flight
in the cries of the night owl

no, you cannot force the poem
it comes when it will
in the softness of a lover's face

with lips of promise
it will lure you to unknown labyrinths
where mind meets mind
where heart's door unlatches
to the blissful, dangerous rush
of limitless space

FALL

fall comes back in our town
blowing crisp wind
on the sunny, yellow mornings of leaves
blushing like golden apples against crystal blue skies

and it's the same beauties accruing onto our paths
the same old dreams we rake

the same ancient maples re-enacting their splendour
in the vestiges of another season

life showing off the best of itself
in the hues of sun and blood

before bowing for the last time
again, on the stage of the world

PREMONITION

on cool, fall mornings
large, white clouds mushroom
like mounds of snow
over Lake Ontario

reminding us
of impending winter

and it's the wind that speaks
its voice a chill
of frozen skies to come
of ice already had

endless stretches of sterility
consciousness clinging
to memories of summer

life's delusions glorified
in the mind's recasting

our life slipping away
as we fend off
another season of ice storms

THIS NEW MORNING

"And yet, there is only one great thing; the only thing: to live, to see, in huts and on journeys, the great day that dawns and the light that fills the world." (Inuit Song)

the pale blue sky draws a tidy line
across the lake's grey eyelid

a seagull planes down
onto the wet pebbles

struts by a stone inukshuk
built yesterday perhaps
by the children playing on the beach
or two lovers maybe
stacking dreams
stone upon stone like kisses

beyond the bark of the old oak tree
a large willow hangs at the edge
caressing the water's paleness
with long, green shimmers

this morning
the benches are witness
to this empty theatre
as my skin is to the shiver of cold wind

I stand here alone
a hazy figure sketched
against the muted colours of this still life canvas
still life
begging to be painted on
with the bold strokes of some new meaning
while behind me
on the busy streets of town
life clanks like a rope of metal cans
rattling beyond all dreams
with its trail of truths and delusions.

THE TWO MUSKOKA CHAIRS

Yesterday,
Searching through a box
Of old photographs,
I remembered
The summer the storm hit.

How it tore the trees
From their very pith.
Knocking them down on roads
And hydro wires. Blocking traffic
Through town. Creating outages.

I remembered how the wind rocked
That rickety cottage, barely anchored
As it was to sand, on railway ties.
All night the rain had pelted the asphalt shingles
Shaking the frail siding to its foundations.

It was a miracle the pine framed window panes held up.
The roof riding it out like an old canoe
With its precious cargo of our children
And us, two disparate oars
Rowing to safety from the storm. Inside.

The next morning while everyone slept
I had gone out in my robe, coffee in hand
To assess the damage. Barefoot
Stepping carefully over the debris
Of acorns, leaves and bark from a fallen oak
Littering the deck and everything.

On the barbecue, shucked from its pivot
The patio umbrella lay back unhinged.
The two Muskoka chairs had made it through
Unscathed. Under soggy, gardenia-rose
Tropical patterned cushions

Beneath a disappearing hue of robin's egg
Blue. Their weathered driftwood stood firm
Like stone. Stoic as wisdoms.

In the distance, from across the water
They must have etched Canada.
Kept watch over its silent face.

Parched with sun and endless snows,
Withstanding it through to the limpid springs
Of cold water lilies floating like open secrets.
Extrapolating light from their long drowned roots.
Deep in Precambrian rock and virgin forests. Loons.

Such dangers cupped in black tea coloured lakes!

I wondered where the passion was then.
Reading Neruda, and love so far away.
Saying what? With whom?

While you inside, scanned the newspaper
From front to back. Planned for retirement.
Watched hockey.

I remember drinking wine
Outside, after putting the kids to bed
And lighting lemon scented luminaries.
Braving the mosquitoes and the black flies
Before the big storm hit.

In the photo, I am young.
In my orange-turquoise sari.
Wild red flip flops. Silver bangles.

I am sitting in one of the two
Empty Muskoka chairs.
My silhouette merging with the growing dark.
Staring at the moon.

SUMMER EVENING

On the opalescent ripples
Of the lake at dusk
Geese are lining up
In haphazard formations
Spelling cryptic meanings
Like black messages in Arabic.

The sky, drunk with summer
Lifts a copper goblet
Into the coming night
Spilling sunset
Onto the dark spine
Of Toronto's skyline
Like so much crumpled tinfoil.

On the other side, darkness
Emits intermittent lights
On and off red
Through the heavy foliage of trees
Nestled along the horseshoe
Hiding the Gotham-like squalor
Of Hamilton's industrial harbour.

Better here alone
On the rocks.
In this hidden, silent cove.
Better here
Under this large, white moon
Healer of my sins.
This communion wafer
Holy moon
Threading an uneven line
From space to me
Across the water
Like the white seagull
Hopping ever closer

On the algae covered stones
At my feet
With its carnivorous beak.
Its flat, fish eye
Calculating to strike,
Perhaps to oust me
As if it sensed
The corpse in me
Like some quantum premonition.

Josie Di Sciascio-Andrews *has published five collections of poetry:* The Whispers of Stones, Sea Glass, The Red Accordion, Letters from the Singularity *and* A Jar of Fireflies. *In 2013, Josie's poetry was shortlisted for Descant's Winston Collins Best Canadian Poem Prize. In 2014, her poem* Emerald City *was shortlisted for The* Malahat Review*'s Open Seasons Award. She has two non-fiction publications* How the Italians Created Canada *and* In the Name of Hockey.

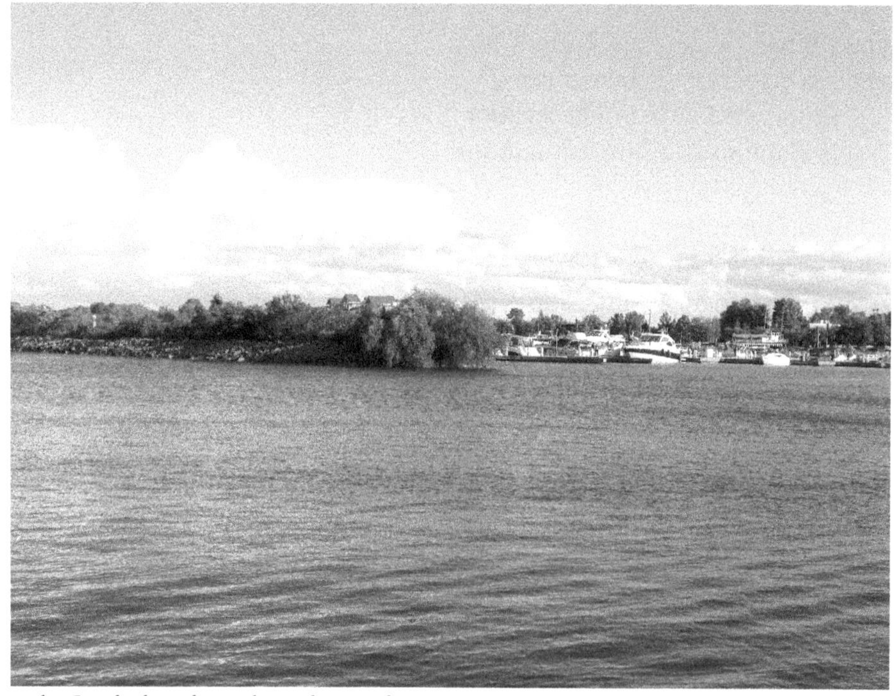

Lake Couchiching by Mahmood Mustafa

Mahmood Mustafa

LAKE COUCHICHING[1]

Breaking the mundane,
The run, the usual …
Stepping out a little from the spotlight,
Finding a getaway
… Far from detection
And giving in to nature … without fuss:
The essence of life … a little life!
The essence of love … a little self!

Lake Couchiching, in its serene majesty,
Its soft, lazy, sleepy waves,
Lapping the shores in rhythmic ripples,
The surrounding forests … a canvas of bright patterns,
And the trees … brushes of an artist …
Stand dripping intense, fiery colors;
And autumn in its seasonal glory
Is in full bloom!

The morning breeze, with a slight nip
Adds freshness to the scene
And the new born sun
Lends brilliance to the surroundings,
And I, incidentally, stand silent and alone,
And witness
This rare kaleidoscope
And accept and count
One more free offering from Nature,
One more blessing added to the umpteen!

(From Crossroads and Beyond *by Mahmood Mustafa, IOWI, 2015)*

1 Lake Couchiching is 16 km long and located in Central Ontario. It is separated from Lake Simcoe by a narrow channel where the city of Orillia is located. The lake is popular for fishing in summer and ice fishing in winter. In autumn, the trees in the area explode in unbelievably vibrant colours.

O CANADA!

I bring richness from the East
And add it to the wealth
Of my home and 'native' land:
O Canada, O Canada!
Our home and native land …
The land of immigrants!

You have been a sanctuary,
A haven, a refuge
To the multitude,
To the millions,
To the clusters diverse
Who flock to you
For admission, for adoption
For settlement:
O Canada, O Canada!
Our home and native land
The land of immigrants!

Your arms open wide
To welcome and embrace
All cultures, all colors,
All creeds and all sects
Who sail to your shores
From numerous lands of the globe
Bringing in turn
Rich knowledge and wisdom,
Strengthening your stream
Of diversity and integration

For many this is journeys' end
And for many more
You provide the launching pad
For future glories, for greater heights,
O Canada, O Canada!
Our home and native land
The land of immigrants!

May you ever prosper
May you always shine
May your fame spread far and wide
And may you remain the beacon
That you always were,
Guiding and welcoming new sons …
Some broken, some shipwrecked,
Some robbed, some dejected …
Who, once rejuvenated,
Will stand on guard for you;
O Canada, O Canada!
Our home and native land,
The land of proud immigrants!

(From Crossroads and Beyond *by Mahmood Mustafa, IOWI, 2015)*

Mahmood Mustafa *was born and raised in India and studied at the prestigious Osmania University in Hyderabad with a focus on English Literature. He continued to be an avid reader in English, Urdu and Hindi literature. Mahmood published two collections of poems in India and* Crossroads and Beyond, *IOWI, 2015, is his first collection published in Canada. He has recited his poetry on radio. His poem* Time *won the Editor's Choice Award and publication in The National Library of Poetry anthology, Owing Mills, Maryland. He lives in Whitby, Ontario.*

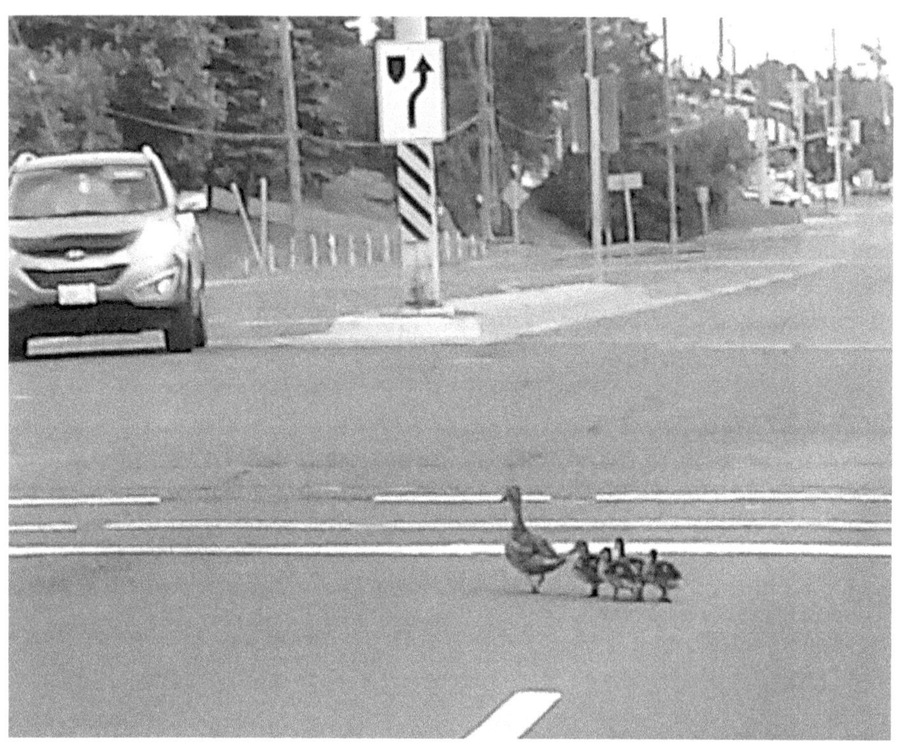

Now That's Canadian by Nadia Tretikov

Nadia Tretikov

NOW THAT'S CANADIAN!

I was hurrying to work in rush hour traffic joining the people going to work from upper York region heading south. I waited in the lineup of cars trying to get off the country road onto Highway 404 towards Toronto. Everybody seemed to be in a hurry, their anxious looks a sign that they were praying there'd be no traffic holdups.

All of a sudden the car in front of me slowed down abruptly to half its original speed and jerked to a stop. I barely had time to hit the brakes. *What was going on?* The question seemed to be on everyone's mind as they craned to see the road ahead. No firetruck sirens, no ambulance speeding by with flashing lights. Just a repetitive squeal of tires echoing from behind as drivers reacted to the sudden halt in traffic and jammed on their brakes.

Strangely, there was no oncoming traffic on the opposite side of the road. The impatience of the people sitting in their cars was palpable. Hands were tossed up in exasperation, wrists flicked over to check the time, and lots of huffing and drumming on steering wheels. The question rising off the scene: *What the f… is going on? Traffic lights not working? Is there an accident up ahead that we can't see?*

I tapped nervously on the steering wheel and scanned through several local news channels on the radio looking for traffic reports. But there was no information on any delays off the 404.

Then suddenly the oncoming traffic got into motion. The cars moved slowly and orderly forward and picked up speed as they passed me. I couldn't wait to see what had caused 'the disaster' that had made me ten minutes late for work.

Now the traffic on my side of the road started up slowly and began moving forward. I moved with the other cars but glanced to the side of the road for a sign of the reason for the holdup.

Aha! Of course! What else could it be?! On my right, waddling down the sidewalk was Mother Goose, gracefully and unhurriedly, leading her goslings to a green stretch of meadow that had a little pond. She paused to check on her offspring, who seemed quite well-behaved, clustered together, and scuttling after her.

A smile broke out on my face and seemed to be mirrored in the faces in every car and of every passerby. Suddenly tension eased, and the anger and frustration of being late for work seemed to visibly die down. Already the story was forming in my mind: *Guess why I'm late? Had to stop for a family of geese crossing the road! Isn't that just so normal a scene on a Canadian road, eh?* And there'll be lots of similar stories from coworkers, with understanding nods and lots of laughter.

Yes, a traffic holdup to make way for wildlife to cross the road – so part of life in Canada!

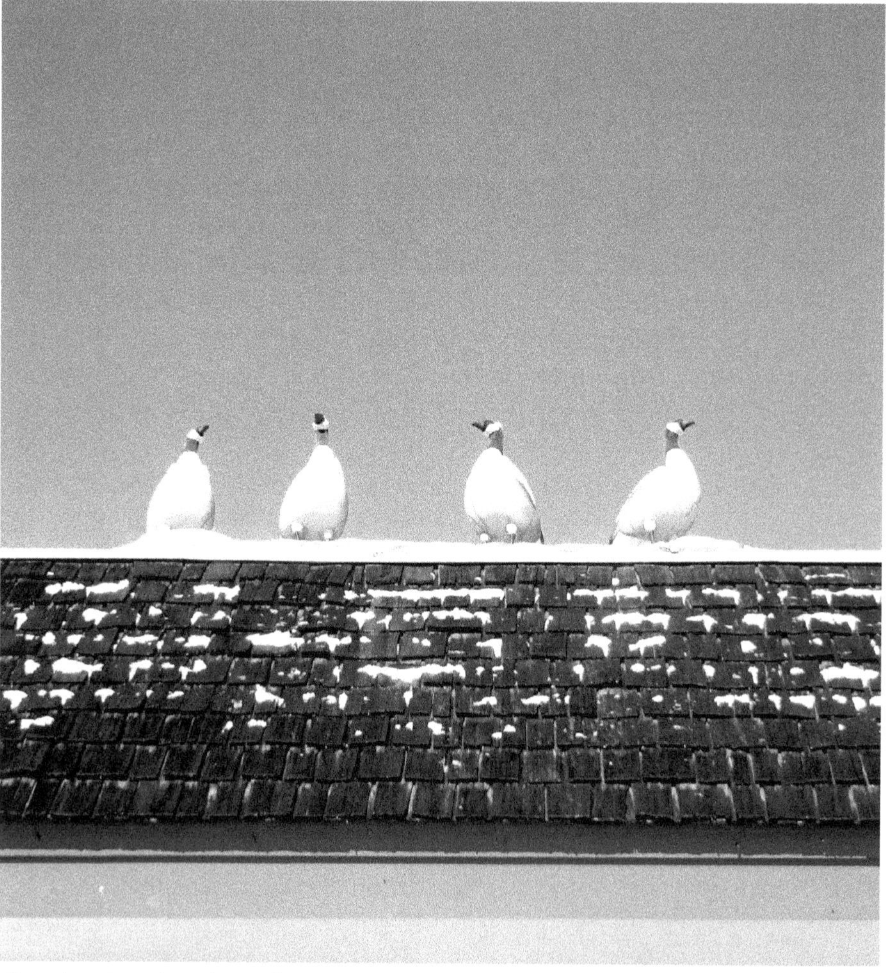

Canadian Guardians by Nadia Tretikov

PROUD TO BE CANADIAN

I sat on the floor near the auditorium where my class was to be held, leaned against the wall, and made myself comfortable. In front of me was a wall of floor to ceiling windows with a view to a courtyard. Students roamed through the yard or sat around in groups or alone, enjoying the warm autumn day.

The sound of voices in excited chatter rose from the direction of the library below and dissipated in the vast open space of the second floor. All around me people were hurrying about, talking, laughing, and sipping coffee from Tim Horton's cups, disappearing in different directions.

Suddenly a few feet away, something red on the ground caught my attention. It was a little Remembrance Day poppy, which had most likely slipped off somebody's jacket lapel. These little red flowers that had bloomed across the battlefields in Flanders during the First World War became a symbol of recognition of the sacrifice of all soldiers who served their country during times of war. Today was 11th of November. It was Remembrance Day in Canada.

I pulled the camera out from my bag and photographed the poppy on the ground. People kept on going up and down the stairs, stepping or jumping over the little poppy flower as it lay on the floor near the stairs. Some cautiously stepped over the poppy, some jumped over it when they saw it, and others simply passed by without even noticing it. But nobody stepped on the flower. It was like a crime scene, with shed blood on the floor. With increasing interest I continued to chronicle "the story of the day" with my camera.

Then a group of students came up the stairs and spread around in front of me. I suddenly noticed that the poppy had disappeared and only a young boy was moving quickly away down the staircase. I rushed after him. He was now by the exit door.

"Excuse me!" I yelled out after him.

He turned around. On the left side of his jacket, close to his heart was my poppy flower.

"May I take a picture of you?" I said, pointing to the poppy. "You rescued it off the ground."

The young lad's face radiated pride as he posed for the photograph.

Both of us felt exactly the same at that moment – proud to be Canadian.

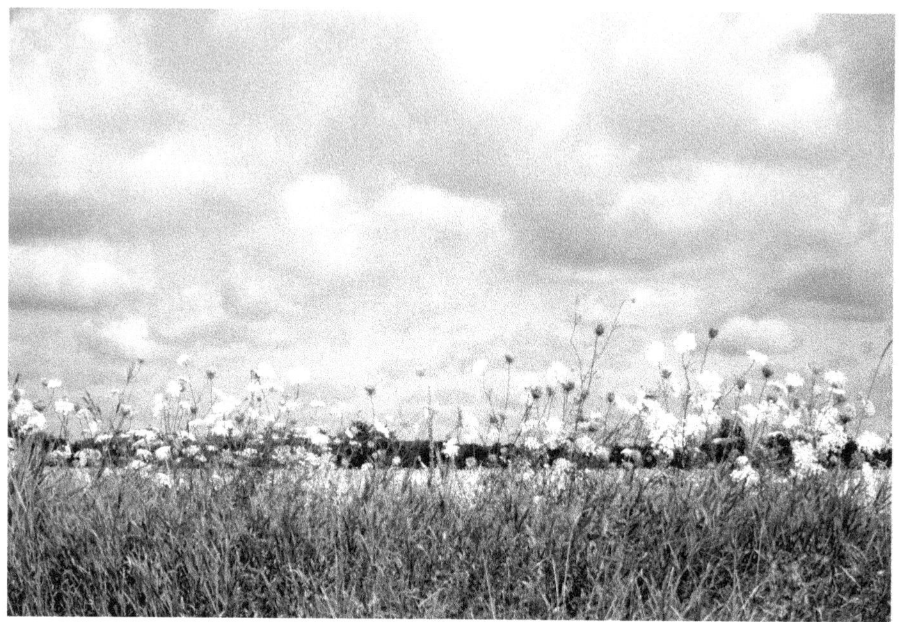

Summer Fields in Canada by Nadia Tretikov

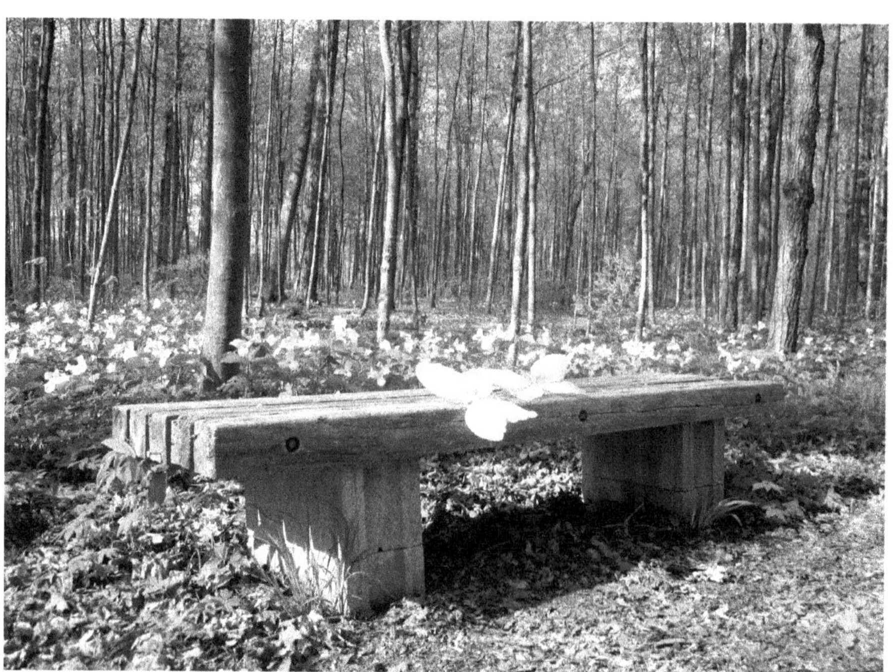

Butterflies and Trilliums by Nadia Tretikov

MARVIN

I forgot the color of your hair,
I forgot the sparkle in your eyes.
I wander through life,
With frozen tears in my heart.

Twenty years—a long time in a person's life …

Marvin lost his wife Liz twenty years ago, when he was fifty-three. By then, their children had grown up. The family had just bought a house in a small town north of Toronto and left a bustling and vibrant area with no regrets.

The eldest son had graduated from the University of Guelph and moved to Manitoba to work as a wildlife biologist. He was very pleased with his work and called home often. The younger son was studying art and design at the University of Toronto. He had a job, shared a small downtown apartment with his friend, and showed up at least once a month. Julia, their daughter, had just entered York University to study child psychology. Despite the fact that the university was far from their new location, she chose to stay with her parents. She traveled early in the morning at half past six, and often returned late at night, doing homework in the library or at a friend's.

Marvin was proud of his children. They have gotten along well with their mother. After the birth of their first child, his wife left her job. They decided that it would be better for everyone. Liz missed the work atmosphere sometimes, but she loved children and her husband more. And Marvin gave her every opportunity to practice her favorite hobbies. Liz loved to draw, knit, and embroider.

From time to time she attended different clubs, and sometimes even participated in local exhibitions. Marvin loved his wife very much. For their whole life together he has never reproached her even though sometimes he had to work several jobs at a time.

Marvin worked for a large trading company at that time and was the manager of sales for construction materials. He earned decent money, but their costs of living were too high. Friday and Saturday nights he worked part-time in the warehouse, and sometimes even helped his friend to install windows and doors.

Liz spent all day, morning to evening, with the children. When Julia was a baby, it was especially hard. Their parents could not help. There was no personal life at all. The boys grew up noisy and mischievous. After school they both attended swimming and karate classes. They always bombarded him with broken bikes, transformers and Lego games, excitedly telling him their news.

Julia was a wonderful child: calm and affectionate. He especially loved her. As a child, she would hug him, putting her little hands around his neck, kissing him and saying, "I love you Daddy!"

Marvin loved these memories. Despite all the difficulties, those were the happiest years.

Then, Liz fell ill totally unexpectedly. She was diagnosed with leukemia, and passed away shortly after. This happened one year after they had moved to the new home. There were so many plans for home improvements. The house had been bought very cheap, even though it was a very nice place, quiet, near the park and the lake. Now the area had grown and a large shopping center had been constructed nearby. Twenty years ago it had only been a small residential area on the outskirts of the city...

Marvin sat on the porch and enjoyed the solitude of the view. He had changed a lot during these twenty years, had gotten older of course, but that was not the reason for the big change in him. From a very strong, vibrant and active middle-aged man, he had become a silent and indolent elderly man. After the death of Liz, he could often be seen in the tavern, where he would stay late for the company.

Although Marvin had never abused alcohol before, you could see more empty vodka bottles around the house. His sons first tried to distract him with their life's problems and interests, but all their attempts were unsuccessful—the father showed no sign of interest. He kept to himself.

Even with his daughter Julia, Marvin mostly remained silent, though he still listened to her stories of the family, friends and neighbours. When Julia asked for help with anything, he helped readily, but silently, with no manifestation of enthusiasm or joy. Julia worked in a school nearby and often dropped home for dinner. Marvin did all the housework himself. Despite the fact that he was in his seventies, he never asked for help with household chores.

He had no interest in women either. After Liz' death, he never even tried to start a relationship with someone new. At first, relatives and friends invited him to visit—for Christmas dinner or lunch on Thanksgiving Day, but every time Marvin found an excuse to cancel the date. Gradually, he distanced himself from everyone.

Marvin kept on asking himself the same question: *What did I do wrong? Why did Liz leave me so early?* He blamed himself.

He blamed himself for a life that was difficult; blamed himself for working all the time; blamed himself for not having spent more time together; that they had never gone on a vacation.

After Liz's death, his life seemed to stop. As time went on, he missed her more and more, trying to recapture the past, which was impossible.

After the funeral, Marvin started driving to the cemetery almost every day, returning home late and immediately going to sleep. Julia started to worry. His sons came over, but nothing helped. Marvin said that he was all right, silently walked out, got into his car and drove to the cemetery.

He would 'talk to Liz,' sitting on the ground near the small modest cross on her grave. He talked about the past, starting with their first date and trying to remember every detail. At times he remembered something new and hastened to tell her about it.

Eventually he only visited the cemetery on weekends, then once or twice a month. This went on while he was still working. When Marvin retired, he spent evenings in the pub. He spoke to nobody; he either watched sports on television or listened to what others were talking about. Employees and patrons of the pub always said a friendly "hello" or "bye" to him—he became a familiar presence.

Two or three times a year his children tried to be at home together. Sometimes they managed to do it, sometimes not. The eldest son got married and had two children, a girl and a boy. There was no big wedding; the couple spent a week on a cruise in Europe, freeing their father of unnecessary hassle.

When the grandchildren came over to visit, Marvin stayed at home. He didn't speak much, but perhaps it was the only time when you could see a smile on his face. The middle son still lived alone and Julia also. The atmosphere in the house was still stretched: conversations felt awkward, there were a lot of hidden questions, hints and looks. Julia had boyfriends, but as soon as the relationship took a serious nature, she immediately stopped seeing them and would sit at the computer or watch TV in the evenings.

Twenty years passed and Marvin still had not found an answer to his question.

Then one day while he was sitting on the porch and enjoying the world go by, a woman came out of the house across the street, started her car and drove off. Marvin had noticed her before. She appeared to be a little younger than him, was always neatly dressed, with beautifully coiffed hair. Sometimes he saw her playing outside the house with her grandchildren.

At the sight of her, Marvin always thought of Liz. And now as he watched the departing car he remembered how quickly and nimbly Liz gathered the children to go to school. Suddenly the car turned around and drove straight to his house. The woman rolled down her window and waved. Marvin got up and slowly walked over to the car. They had never spoken before today; just waved to each other.

"Marvin's your name, isn't it?" she said. "Our grandchildren sometimes play with each other. I hate to ask you this like this, but we've been neighbours for so many years! I'm going to the club. I really need to have a partner tonight. Please, say you will come with me," she laughed. "I'll tell you everything along the way."

Marvin got confused. What? Where? In a club? With this woman? If it were Liz...

"Well," he said to his own surprise, "I will just change and come back."

The woman was waiting in the car. Five minutes later, Marvin was back. He had put on his dark-coloured summer trousers and a blue tennis shirt with short sleeves. It was a warm summer evening. He sat down beside her in the car and she drove off.

"My name is Chelsea. My husband died a few years ago. I don't live far away, but during the week I come here to help my daughter with her children. I love the kids! I do nothing all day anyway. It's good for the children, and I don't feel so alone.

Tonight there is a 'White Dance.' Everyone will have a partner. I didn't find anybody, and then I saw you and thought, "Why not?" Thank you for accepting. I promise you'll like it. I have been going there for about five years. I had a dance partner, but he recently got married and I was left on my own ..." The woman laughed again.

They drove through familiar streets and soon stopped at a two-storey building in a small plaza. The sign read: "Emma's Dance Club." At the entrance stood baskets with flowers. During the ride Marvin did not say a word. It was like a dream. He let the woman go in first.

There were beautiful light silver-blue curtains on the windows and in the left corner alongside the wall there was a long table covered with a white tablecloth and laden with plates of sandwiches, fresh fruit and vegetables. On a small table next to it there were jars with juices, pop and water. People in small groups were scattered around the room. On a small platform against the far right wall the musicians were tuning their instruments.

Chelsea led her new companion to one of the groups and introduced him to her friends. Marvin smiled awkwardly, but remained silent. *Is this happening to me?* he kept asking himself. People in the audience were almost the same age as him: some were a little younger, some were older. The abrupt sounds of a guitar broke the stillness in the room.

A singer came to the microphone and began to sing. This was a popular country song that Marvin knew. Liz and he had loved this song. A few couples went to the center of the room and danced to the music. Chelsea looked at Marvin and held out her hand …

When Marvin came home, he could not really explain where he had been to Julia, but only awkwardly waved his hand and went to his room. In the morning, he woke up, washed his face, got dressed, and began to work on the house. When Julia came downstairs to the dining room, there was a hot plate waiting for her and the coffee maker was greeting her with cheerful puffing noises. Marvin was smiling.

"Good morning, Julia! Somehow you're late today. Aren't you late?"

Julia couldn't even guess at what had happened last night, but she smiled at him and in her heart she felt relieved and happy. Her father stood before her cheerful and friendly. Julia ate, then promised him to return from work early, and left.

Marvin looked out of the window. Then he put on a cap, took his clippers and went into the garden. He felt energetic—life had returned to him and he wanted to do stuff around the house. That's just how Liz had seen them in their old age, helping their children, meeting with friends at the club, traveling, going to the theater.

Liz, he said to himself, *I remember everything, my dear, I have not forgotten.*

Nadia Tretikov *was born in the Ukraine and came to Canada in 1998. She followed her passion for painting, photography, and writing by taking courses at Seneca College in Toronto. Since 2003, she has published poems and short stories in Russian through Toronto Media, including one thriller* The Running Elephants, *in 2009; and in English in* The Literary Connection Volume I, *2014.*

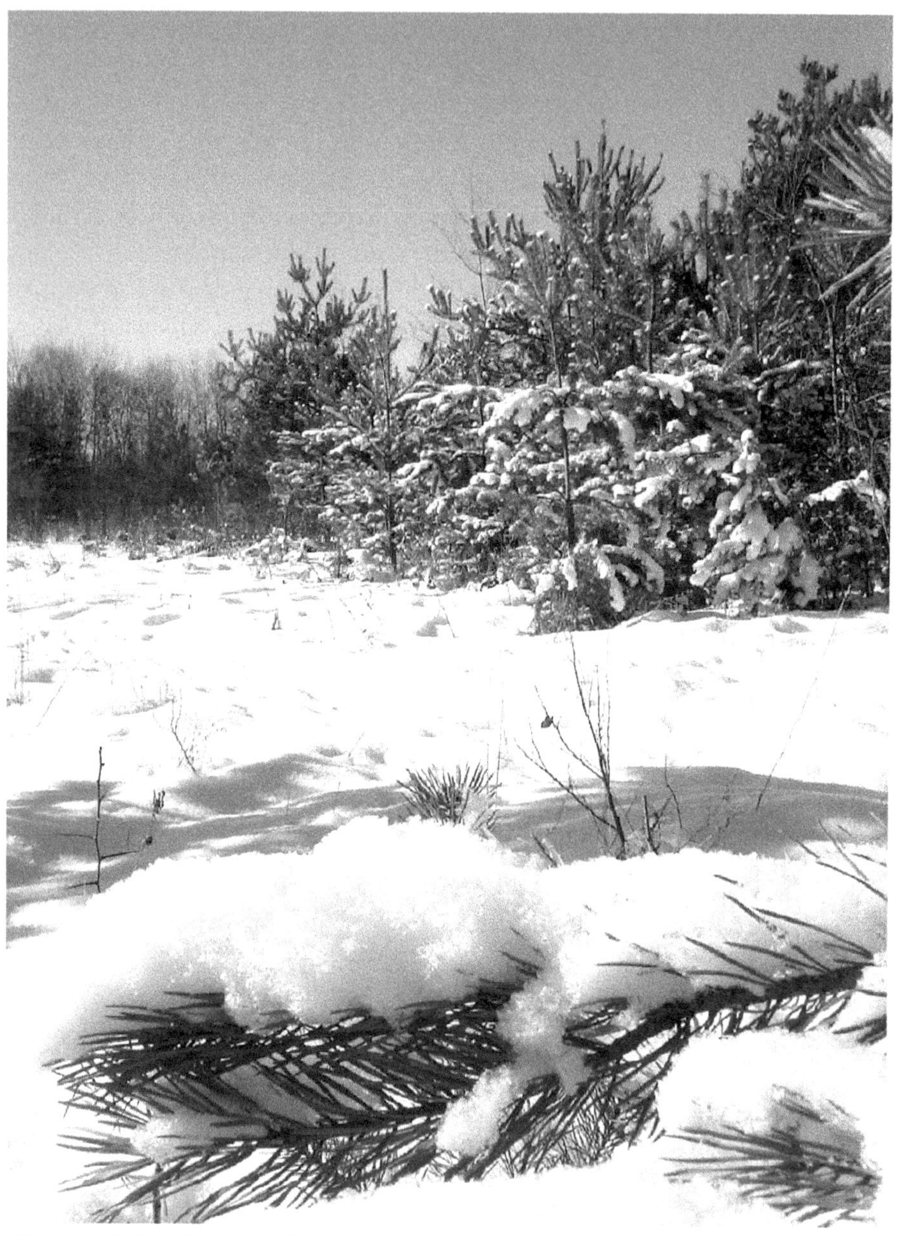

Winter in Oak Ridges by Nadia Tretikov

Peter Jailall

WHY I WRITE

I write
To excavate my past
And to chisel a peephole
Into Canadian living.
Trying to understand.

I write
To purify my soul
And to heed the cries
Of injustice
Ignored by power hungry politicians

I write
To bleed bad blood
And to suffer with sufferers
Challenging the unmoved
To heed their cries.

I write
To learn
And I write, for me.

(From This Healing Place and other poems, *Natural Heritage Books, 1993)*

REFAGEE

Dem dribe me out
A me own countree
Prapa treet me baad
Mek me cum way hay
Wan refagee
Wid bad money

Dem Kanaydian tek me in
In dem own countree
Prapa treet me gud
Wen me cum dung hay
Mek me wan citizen
Dem own picknie, wid rights
An human dignity.

Refugee
They drove me out
Of my own country
Treated me bad
Made me go away
A refugee
With bad money

Canadians took me in
In their own country
Treated me well
When I came here
Made me a citizen
Their own child, with rights
And human dignity.

(From This Healing Place and other poems, *Natural Heritage Books, 1993)*

THE LONELY IMMIGRANT

Here I come
Hustling down
For the early morning subway train
All decked out
In me cheap pinstripe
Looking at them
To see how I look
Why don't they look at me?
Hey man,
I've just arrived
To this promised land
Trying my best
To look like one of you
Flapping my suit
In the winter breeze
Straightening my shoulders
Lifting my head up high
Compressing my lips
Trying my best
To make me mouth look nice
Saying "Nice day, eh?"
Jiving with the Yonge Street crowd,
Fooling no one
I'm just a force-ripe
Hyphenated Canadian

(From This Healing Place and other poems, *Natural Heritage Books, 1993)*

NO MORE TERRIFYING GAZE

In the heat
Of the Guyanese canefields
Those blue eyes of steel
Melted me down
And drove fear
In me coolie soul.

But not now,
After I settled here
In these fields of frozen snow
I have become a fearless Canadian
With equality, dignity and courage.

(From Sacrifice—poems on the Indian arrival in Guyana, *In Our Words Inc. 2010)*

LETTER TO KAMALA-JEAN

Like you,
I wanted details.

The name of the ship.
The meaning of my name
The origin of my ancestors.
Details.
Of their punishment,
Humiliation,
Death.
Knowledge
Of how they were treated,
Of how they were hated.

Children jeered:
"Coolie Gal, your ancestors
Arrived at Port Royal
With tails like monkeys
Which had to be cut off"

You are
Jamaican East Indian West Indian Indo Caribbean
Canadian.

Like you, I am not only East-Indian—
I'm Guyanese, Caribbean and Canadian,
Visible with a voice.
We have many identities.

Now I know
No more Coolie Gal,
But dignified woman—
Intelligent
And strong.

MEENA'S TREASURES

Among her precious pieces of gold
At the bottom of her black suitcase
Wrapped tightly in a brown paper bag
Meena brought seeds, *poi bhajee* seeds
To transplant her agri-culture
On cold Canadian soil.

But on arrival, she first settled in an apartment
So she planted a small portion of her seeds
In a box on her balcony.
The *bhajee* plants flourished
Thick, green leaves sprung
From Meena's green thumb
She cooked the *poi bhajee* with shrimps
On top of *dhall* and rice
Just like she did
Back in the ole country.

Peter Jailall *is a retired teacher, poet and storyteller. He has published eight books of poetry and nonfiction,* Children like to write; Improve Language Instruction; When September Comes; Yet Another Home; This Healing Place and Other Poems; Mother Earth: Poems for Her Children; Sacrifice: Poems on the Indian Arrival in Guyana; *and* Jottings—a Teacher's Logbook. *Peter volunteers with CUSO as a teacher-trainer in Guyana. He received the 2010 Guyana Cultural Association Award for his work in Rural Education in Guyana and in 2011 received the Marty's Award for Established Literary Arts in Mississauga.*

Natalee Johnson

THE BEAUTY OF CANADA ...

The beauty one sees, so hard to describe
Of a country where many have chosen to reside
A Charter that freedom and rights' inscribe.

The maple banner Red and White
Stands for honour, valour, battle might
For peace and freedom and all that's right

A country that champions diversity
Whose policies underscore its humanity
Where dreams become reality.

In Canada … the beauty one sees
Beyond scenic, it's what the heart perceives
Love, peace, kindness … that's the beauty one sees.

HIGH PARK PANTOUM

Let me tell you about a place I know
Where nature steals into one's thoughts
It's an invigorating place to go
Love will enter the heart

Where nature steals into one's thoughts
As family and friends leisurely stroll
Love will enter the heart
It's a peaceful place that will beguile

As family and friends leisurely stroll
The beauty of nature silently teaches
It's a peaceful place that will beguile
While hearts hold memories that won't be lost

The beauty of nature silently teaches
It's an invigorating place to go
While hearts hold memories that won't be lost
Let me tell you about a place I know

(High Park is located in Toronto, Ontario)

Natalee Johnson *immigrated to Canada with her family at the age of five. As a single mother, Natalee traced her journey in a collection of poems entitled* I Come As I am—reflections in verse, *In Our Words Inc., 2012. She is an author, educator, Child and Youth Care worker, and entrepreneur, who is passionate about influencing the lives of other people.*

P. I. Kapllani

JUSTICE AT THE HAGUE

As a ten-year-old boy, Ermal Bllaca fled the city of Gjakova in Kosovo, upon witnessing the killing of his mother and three sisters by the Serbian Police Patrol. The patrol was led by Dragan Spasic, who was their neighbour. In the aftermath of NATO airstrikes over former Yugoslavia in 1999, Ermal's family and other Kosovo Albanians were targeted by Serbian troops as part of a massive ethnic cleansing. The Serbian operation in Gjakova was called "The Horseshoe."

When the attack began, Ermal barely escaped from the basement hideout, where twenty-one women and children were later gunned down. Ermal had a bullet in his arm, but managed to join the human wave of refugees, numbering a million, who fled to neighboring countries. He reunited with his father Adem in the military hospital in Tirana, Albania.

The Bllacas' house in Gjakova was burned to the ground in the raid and with nowhere else to go, Ermal and Adem seek refuge in Canada. In their new country, they start a new life, while still struggling with the ghosts of the past. News from Kosovo keeps them and thousands of Kosovo refugees tied to the media. They learn that after 78 days of NATO airstrikes, the Serbian army and police vigilantes escaped to Serbia. Most devastating is the news that Dragan Spasic and others from the death squads, who had murdered their family in the mass killings and caused the exodus of hundreds of thousands of refugees had themselves escaped justice and found safe haven in Serbia proper.

Two years later, Ermal Bllaca, as the sole surviving witness to the massacre in Gjakova, receives a summons from The Hague Tribunal to testify against former Yugoslavian president Slobodan Milosevic. Ermal, as a 12-year-old minor, is accompanied by Adem to The Hague.

Months later, Milosevic dies in a prison cell. Dragan Spasic and other chetnik warlords are still at large in Serbia and elsewhere. The Bllacas know that justice was not done.

Adem finds new love with Vjollca, but his young son continues to live in the past, his heart full of anger and revenge. Fifteen years pass, but he has not found peace. He is tormented by ghosts of the past, who rise from the grave and implore justice. In his unquiet mind, Ermal starts thinking about taking retribution with his own hands. Unknown to his father he began making plans. He started learning the Serbian language, surfed the internet for information related to the whereabouts of Dragan Spasic and others involved in the massacre in Kosovo.

Finally, he tracked down his family's killer. He located Spasic in Serbia, where he is a hunter of wild boar. Ermal decided to learn hunting as a 'cover.' He practiced hunting and joined the Serbian Canadian Hunting Association. He frequented Serbian night bars in Toronto and found a Serbian girlfriend. He stole the passport of a Serbian Canadian and bought blue-tinted contact lenses to resemble the photo in the passport. He booked a flight to Serbia through the Serbian hunting association.

Adem and his cousin Arben found out about Ermal's plan and joined him in the hunt for the war criminals.

On the hunting field of Stara Planina, Ermal had an emotionally charged moment when he faced his mother and sisters' killer. Dragan Spasic was enjoying life and freedom as a boar hunter, while his victims in exile suffered with hellish memories of his making.

Ermal takes Spasic hostage and struggled to bring him before a EULEX court in Kosovo, but Spasic escaped. His Serbian cohorts put Ermal's life in danger, but Arben and Adem intervened and saved him.

The hunt for Spasic went on, until he was tracked down once more, in Australia.

(From a synopsis of a novel based on actual facts. Ermal Bllaca is a fictional name given to the actual witness of the Kosovo massacre mentioned in the story, who was summoned to The Hague to stand witness against Slobodan Milosevic. The ten-year-old boy fled to Ottawa and still lives there today. He is a grown man, but is still haunted by his memories.)

Përparim Kapllani (P.I.Kapllani) *was born in the city of Elbasan, Albania. He is the author of four books in the Albanian language. His English books include* The Last Will, *a novel based on the Çamëria genocide, 2013.* Beyond the Edge, *a collection of short stories, 2010; the English version of his play* Queen Teuta of Illyria *in 2008 and its Albanian version in 2014. His short stories appear in three anthologies:* Canadian Voices, The Literary Connection, *and* The Courtneypark Connection. *His novella* The Hunter *was shortlisted in The Ken Klonsky novella contest in 2015.*

Susan Munro

I HAVE KNOWN YOU

There is a feeling
        came only once
an abrupt awakening
        that settled over like a shroud
I have known you

Carried over millennia
        tears cried alone
        pain of loss
        memory of love
softness   of entwinement

I now brush past your life
        like an autumn breeze
        carrying my heart
        like a weightless leaf
scurrying to the ground

Covered over with winter snow
            that sleeps,
  sleeps   forever in the cold
              under an icy blanket
              of painful silence

You don't remember
    but I have known you

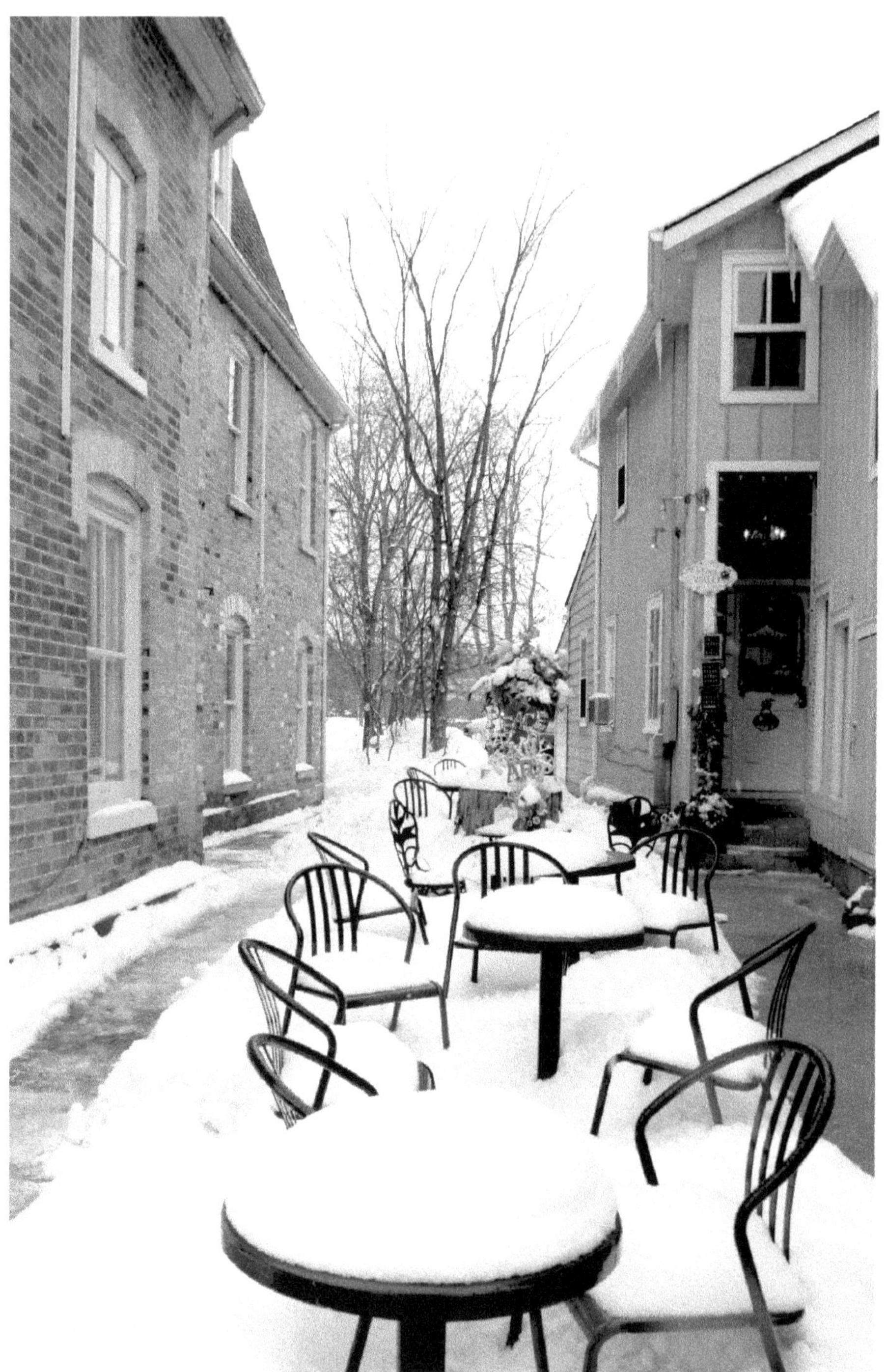

Winter in Markham by Nadia Tretikov

PREPARATION

body aches
after tree branches
trimmed
grass cut
one last time
vines unravelled
hose untangled
detached
railings
re-nailed
secured against
winds that
will blow cold
and icy
moaning
with injustice
at loss of
sunlight
and resignation
that soon
a white cover
will be pulled
over Autumn
to sleep
another Winter

Susan Munro *is a Toronto-based Registered Acupuncturist and Energy Healer. She has studied Esotericism for over 30 years, including Qabalah, Tarot, the Golden Dawn, the Tree of Life and Mysticism. She has published two collections of poems:* Coil *and* Ravings of a Lunatic Saint.

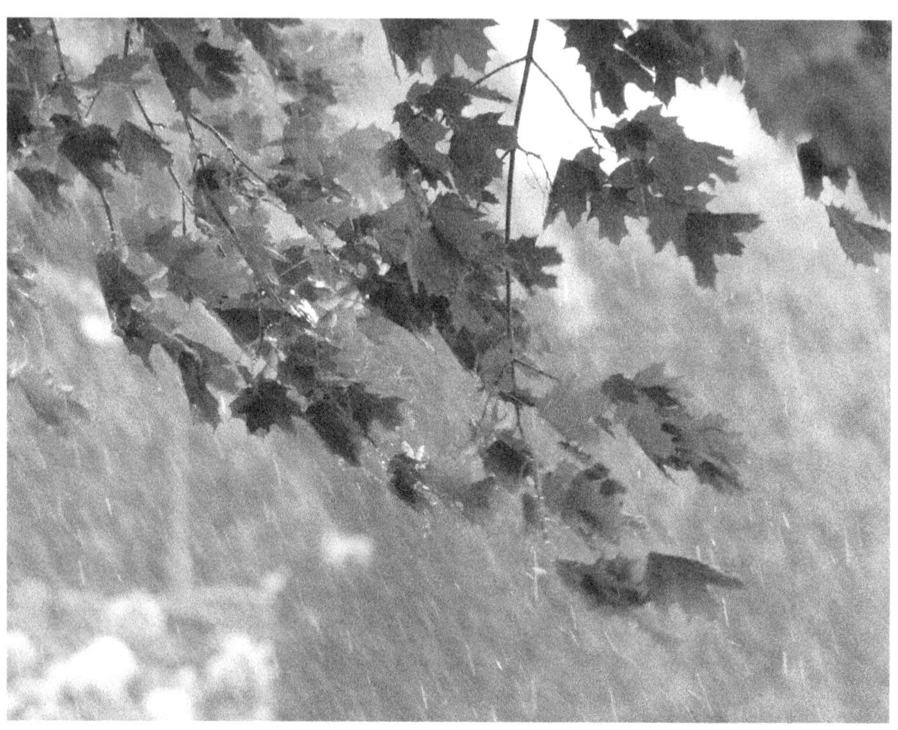

Heavy Rain on Maples by Nina Munteanu

Wayne Croning

FAREWELL AND HELLO

Something told me, kept nagging at me, in fact tormented me for years after. I had this strange and sad feeling that we would never meet again. Inside I was crying my heart out. We had known each other for many years. I had fallen in love and could not let go. She had accepted me as I was, and I her. Yet there seemed to be no love lost on her side when I said I was leaving.

"Go if you must! See if I care! Go if it makes you happy!" She never said these words, but I could see it in her eyes; no, feel it in my bones.

I never turned to look back. It was early July as I boarded the plane with my mom. We were headed to Canada, to a new life, a new country; to be united with my brother Ralph. Mom, Ralph and I had always been together, through thick and thin. It was late at night as the plane ascended into darkness. Gazing out the window, I caught my last glimpse of her, glinting in the still night, so beautiful to look at from way up.

"Goodbye Karachi! I will miss you. I will never forget you!" I promised her in my mind.

The trip to Canada was long and tiring It included a stopover in Frankfurt where we got to meet my aunt and cousin for just thirty minutes and then took a connecting flight via Air Canada direct to Toronto.

At last we arrived in Toronto, Canada, my new country, my new home. We were interviewed by an immigration officer at the airport.

"Are you married?" he asked me.

"No."

"Do you have any children?" he asked me.

"No, I am not married," I replied surprised.

"You don't have to be married to have children," was his polite reply.

"Welcome to Canada," he added, handing me my passport back.

"Welcome to Canada!" Oh how those words warmed my heart!

In the time taken to attend this formal interview, we missed our connecting flight to Winnipeg. We were lucky to get the next connecting flight and to top it off got to travel first class, the only available seats left.

Finally, we landed in Winnipeg and it had just stopped raining. It was cool for July, just 18 C. Ralph and my cousin had come to pick us up in two cars. We loaded suitcases and drove to our new home in the suburbs of St. James. The first thing that stood out for me on that first drive home was the orderly traffic. There was no honking, no jostling around at intersections. NO PEOPLE on the roads, not like in Karachi. I observed a few people strolling along the walkways, but none of the crowds, no throngs of wall-to-wall people I was used to.

The houses were made of wood and reminded me of the beach huts along Karachi's Sandspit and Hawksbay beaches. I was tired, suffering from jet lag and a bad sore throat; something that always happens to me on long journeys. After eating our first meal, I just collapsed.

Next evening I ate my first Big Mac burger under the shade of a shelter at a local park. The air was cool and we took a drive downtown towards St. Boniface and I got my first glimpse of the Red River. A strong icy wind was blowing off her choppy waters. It was freezing cold now. Later, I came to learn that some volcano had erupted in the Philippines blocking the sun's rays for months due to the ash spewed into the upper atmosphere, resulting in a cooling effect in most parts of the world.

The next three weeks were spent exploring Winnipeg, the malls, the parks and local library. After this, my cousin offered me a part time job at a local restaurant where he worked as Kitchen Manager. It was different working here with mostly high school kids working evening shifts. I worked as a prep cook and dishwasher. This was a start and the work was hard and messy. They barely gave me 12-16 hours per week on average and full time is considered 40 hours per week. I was paid minimum wage, which was $5 an hour at that time.

Canada was in a deep recession. There were no jobs available and for a newly arrived immigrant like myself, close to impossible to find full time work.

I did not enjoy working in that restaurant and later managed to get another part time job at a small retail outlet closer to home at a nearby mall. Basically unloading/loading trucks, stocking shelves, etc. It was mundane, backbreaking work, but I got my first big cheque from here and blew it all in a couple of days. They finally laid me off and I ended up working for a small family-run restaurant full time with minimum wage. Much as I hated working at restaurants, I actually ended up working here for two to three years, leaving once for Edmonton in search of work on the oil rigs. There was no luck with this venture.

Three years after immigrating to Canada, mom and I, and about a hundred other people stood before a high court judge at a citizenship ceremony. Proud Canadians, we stood and sang "O Canada" with pride. What a special day! One that I can never forget. At the back of my mind I saw our past flashing by; our life in Pakistan, our quest for a new homeland, the adjusting to a new way of life, the brutal Winnipeg winters. I had no regrets. Canada was truly my home now. I belonged to her and she to me. We were one!

I sometimes meet Asian immigrants and often hear them say "back home" referring to the country where they originally came from and wonder why they still use this term. I would rather use the term "the old country" as Canada is where I live now. I do miss the old country, but Canada is my new home now. I cannot live in two homes at the same time.

Two years later, I finally got a slightly higher paying full time job at a locally run charitable organization. Wow! Six bucks and hour with full benefits. I actually liked this job, working as a handyman. It was while working here that I met and married my wife Sylvia, a pretty girl originally from South India, who was living in Maryland, U.S.A. Sylvia was introduced to me by my late aunt Irene.

I stayed with the organization for five years and finally got laid off, right after finding out that we were expecting our first child. A few weeks after this, I got two job offers, one was at a cold storage facility and the other was at a plastics factory, both paying $10 an hour to start. I took the factory job. Sixteen years later I have no regrets, the hours are long, it includes shift work, but it is rewarding in the end.

Is Canada then 'the land of opportunity'? Is it the 'best country in the world' (to live in)? Am I happy to be here? Am I proud to call myself a Canadian (citizen)? I answer with an emphatic YES to all questions. I have no regrets.

Canada offers a lot of opportunity. Immigrants have been pouring in for over two hundred years from all four corners of the world. It is a country of immigrants. We must respect the original inhabitants of this great nation. May we all continue to strive together to better not only our nation, but the world in general.

I miss the 'old country.' Maybe someday I may visit.

Oh Canada! Proud to be Canadian.

Wayne Croning *is the author of* Karachi Backwaters *and several short stories, one of which was published in a magazine called Anglos in the Wind. Born and educated in Karachi, Pakistan; he immigrated to Canada in the early 90s and works and lives with his wife and two children in Winnipeg. History, boating, reading and writing are his main hobbies.*

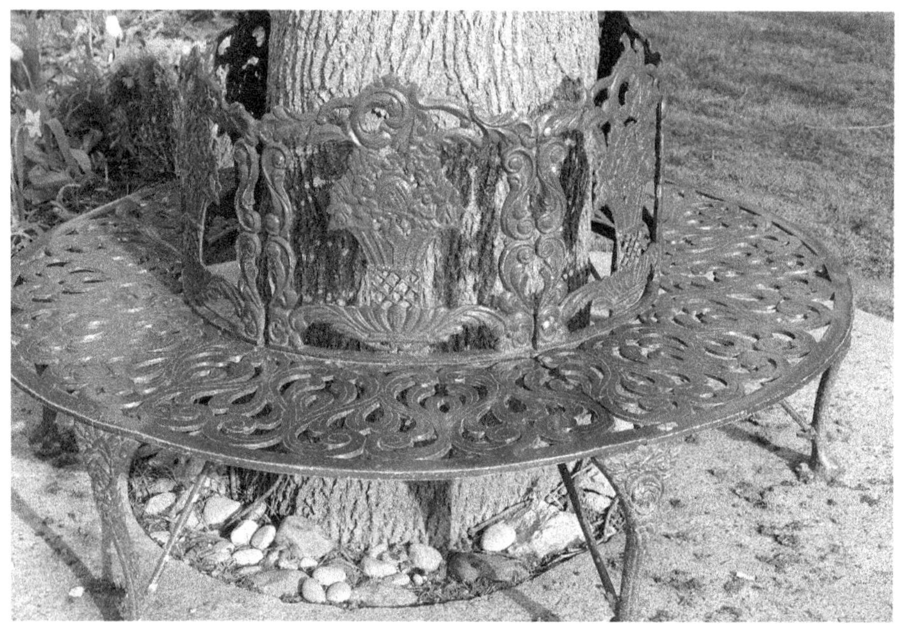

Bench and Tree Trunk by Merridy Cox-Bradley

Zohra Zoberi

IMMIGRANT WOMAN

She most likely had no say
in the decision to migrate
thousands of miles
away from her siblings, parents and friends
Used to walking two steps behind
expected to tag along, so she did

New climate free from suffocation
opportunities unlimited
Putting her best foot forward
she's able to walk
two steps ahead

Migration of thousands of miles
did not deserve as much credit
as those four steps
she has taken
on her own

Oh, but now …
she must struggle
to take two steps back
in order to remain in line

(From True Colours *by Zohra Zoberi, IOWI, 2012)*

THERE'S A ROOM FOR YOU

Replica
of our global village
there's a special room
where east meets west
north greets south and …
light dispels darkness:
    Through the dark corridor
    you spiral
    down the mysterious stairway
    where one 'descends' in order to
                                        'ascend'

where musicians play happy melodies
poets recite verses, in many languages
this exclusive venue is 'inclusive'
of all races
multi-coloured faces

    Where ordinary people come to perform
    extraordinary deeds
    A symbol of perfect harmony
    no stereotyping
    true bonding
    interracial
    interfaith and intercultural
    This is where people from all walks of life
    converge, creativity for a common cause:
  "Enlightenment through entertainment"

While solving and
resolving issues
commonalities discovered
Differences recognized
diversity celebrated
many a gap we continue to bridge
common Canadian values we seek

The magic of our multicultural mosaic
Christians, Muslims and Jews
Sikhs and Hindus
whites, blacks, and browns
people in sarees, sarongs and kimonos
mingled with those in skirts and blue jeans
Hand in hand;
Polish, Chinese, Italian, Romanian, Filipino
of many other origins
United Nations truly 'united.'
How we relished our meals
of Shami kebab, Italian Pizza, Szechwan noodles
sushi, perogies and the falafel
a potluck of food
and folk

One way this 'Replica' differs from
the rest of the world we may proudly say:
harmony exists!
This is a room
where you bring your basket in
empty it and refill
till it overflows

"No matter what colour you are
tears are all the same"
laughter alike
The 'I' less significant
'us' is a bigger
plus …
there is room for you
It all began …
in the basement of my home

BECOMING A CANADIAN

"What brings people to Canada?" The assumption is that people leave their struggles behind to find a free and more comfortable life, but there are exceptions. Some of us pay a heavy price to achieve this freedom.

I was probably ten or eleven when I met a newly-wed young lady who was about to fly to Canada to start a new life. *Canada*? I had looked it up in the Atlas and saw that it was the farthest point from Pakistan. "Maybe one day," I thought, "I too could venture there." I was impressed by her bravery, but it was the various sizes of bright red luggage that fascinated me. I was a long way from realizing the impact her *baggage* had on me.

Having enjoyed twelve years as the wife of a prestigious Professor in Nigeria at a university campus referred to as *Mini-America*, it wasn't an easy decision. We would be giving up an annual three months' paid vacation, a luxurious furnished bungalow, a car and driver, plus servants to pamper us at will and all free of charge. Spoilt, we were.

During a sabbatical in Uppsala University a Canadian colleague asked: "Why would anyone in their right mind abandon such a lifestyle?" Well, we were in our right mind and about to make a major shift.

Stacks of books and atlases were spread across our coffee table for months as we contemplated where our new homeland would be. We studied the possibilities of the USA, Australia, Sweden, Canada and England. My husband had already ruled out any possibility of returning to Pakistan. And since he had spent ten years of his youth in London, I was sure that the U.K. was a possibility. He dismissed that idea with a … *but*! This mysterious '*but*' would eventually become clear, however, at the time, he just said: "It's my gut feeling."

The possibilities continued with England deleted from the list. Australia presented good opportunities in the field of education. A few Professors from our University had secured teaching positions there but their feedback on racism had us rule out Australia. We wanted to be *accepted* not just *tolerated.*

Our friends from Wisconsin University offered some compelling advice: "There's less crime and a slower pace of life in Canada which makes it far better than the USA."

Canada, half way across the globe, was circled in red on the Atlas. *What of the scary distance from our loved ones?* Well, we were young back then, so we didn't realize how the distance could become longer…and longer…and longer as you get older… and older.

Next Steps: Applications and Medical Examinations

With hundreds of people wanting to immigrate to Canada, we were surprised and blessed when two young Canadians from the Immigration Office in Paris, flew to Lagos to interview only two other couples and us. They told us: "You'll need to set aside six months of income for living expenses because that will be the longest period it will take for a scientist with a PhD to find a suitable job."

Back then, the Nigerian Niara was higher than the Canadian Dollar. The substantial dollars we were to bring with us likely raised our qualifying score. We were accepted just like that. In short we had been declared physically, mentally and financially healthy to try and become hyphenated Canadians.

We received our immigration papers with an arrival date. During every discussion about Canada, images of red suitcases flashed through my mind! I had no idea why, but I was compelled to go out and purchase a lovely three-piece ruby red set of luggage before we began packing to leave.

We made stopovers in Vienna and Bonn then flew to London to meet family friends. Professor Kalmus was a highly revered and by then retired Professor who had migrated from Eastern Europe. After a memorable English dinner, I posed my key question to him:

"You are a well-travelled and enlightened individual, what would be your single piece of advice to a young couple migrating to another country?"

"I'm confident you'll know how to handle this challenge; but I would say, mingle with people of all ethnicities. Don't remain in a community ghetto. Adapt."

Arriving in the Land of Opportunity

As I opened my red suitcases for inspection at immigration, a rush of memory came over me. I smiled as I recalled the lovely lady and her red luggage that had so impressed me as a child. Here I was, red luggage and all, entering Canada just like she had; most likely with all the same hopes, fears and dreams she experienced on her arrival.

I wondered if she also found it uncomfortable to have to declare her most personal treasures. I laid the jewelry on the counter for inspection and I thought of my international collection of household items I had sold for *auney pauney* (next to nothing). The only remaining remnant of our pampered past was our Royal Doulton English bone china dinner set… my consolation prize for not whining over all that I had to leave behind.

My Canadian cousins Rani and Riaz offered their place for a few weeks. Their apartment complex in Mississauga was cheekily referred to as the *Taj Mahal* or sometimes more sarcastically as *Paki Palace.*

An urgent search for suitable accommodations superseded our job hunt. Half-decent was our minimum requirement.

Suite 307-3400 Riverspray Crescent, Applewood Hills. The address itself had a musical ring that implied a classy location. I imagined apple orchards and a flowing river nearby.

"There's absolutely no way they'll rent it to us!" was my husband's reaction. By *us*, he meant *us* brown people. He shared with me that he had been refused accommodation in posh areas of London in the sixties which made me suddenly realize why he didn't want to migrate to England! Now I understood the importance of the "gut feeling" he had expressed… and the mystery of the unfinished 'BUT' sentence he had left dangling.

Once our credit rating from British and Swiss banks had been cleared, the apartment keys were handed to us.

My husband had to go back to his fulltime job in Nigeria, at least until a suitable position was available in Canada. Goodbyes are never easy, especially as it meant I would have to struggle on my own in a new country with a six-year-old.

Cardboard boxes neatly covered with Nigerian tie-dyed fabric served as our table. Our furniture, purchased from liquidation sales, was to be delivered later but for the time being a simple mattress on the floor would do fine, as long as my stereo system was nearby to keep me company during my long, lonely, sleepless nights.

In the quiet moments, the wind made scary screeching sounds. I brought in a handyman to fix it. He told me: "The glass doors aren't sealed right so they need cocking." I was shocked to hear that word. *My door needs cocking*?

What in the world could that mean? I was comforted once I looked it up in the dictionary as 'caulking.'

After my six-year-old was tucked into bed each night, DJ Glenn Darling at the Burlington FM station became my evening companion; and this lonely lady soon developed a taste for sappy English songs of the seventies. That announcer's voice remains in the sound box of my memory.

My husband's absence led my heart to green pastures where romantic letters bloomed. He was as miserable without me as I was without him. I had much too much time to kill.

One day I noticed an interesting ad on the bulletin board of a grocery store. People could actually tear the telephone number off the page, take it home and make the call? So I placed my ad on the Dominion Store bulletin board.

New comers!
Women only!
Learn English in the comfort of a welcoming home.
Socialize while you utilize your time
Charges are minimum and negotiable.

Within a week I had lined up several elderly Portuguese, Italian, and Polish women to enroll with me. I set the price at only $8 per hour and no one even tried to bargain.

Once my husband returned from Nigeria, he faced the harsh reality of job hunting with disappointment after disappointment. Finally, one day he broke some good news.

"I got it, I got the job. I finally got the job! But it's not exactly here in Toronto."

"Wonderful! As long as it's not in the Prairies."

He accepted a temporary position as a visiting Professor in the Microbiology Department of the University of Regina. The Prairies! I consoled myself with the word temporary.

The Temporary Manpower Services found me a three-week assignment to work with the Task Force on Canadian Unity in Regina. Being from a family that had suffered the consequences of the India/Pakistan partition and migration; and again in Nigeria, living through the cessation attempt of Biafra, it seemed ironic that many years later the country I would choose would also be entangled in language and cultural conflicts. Quebec independence was on everyone's mind.

I was later invited to an interview with the Director of Community Colleges. A tall gentleman, in his early fifties, walked into the office to shake hands with nervous little me.

Bismillah Al Rehmanirraheem. I begin with the name of Allah… or God was an automatic thought for me.

As he glanced at my resume, I summoned up the courage to confess: "In Toronto, my Placement Officer recommended that I should delete two items from my resume… but I, um, I haven't, um, done that."

"And what might those be?" He asked.

"Um, that my schooling was in Pakistan… and… that I had… three gold medals to my credit."

"So, why didn't you delete them?" His friendly curiosity was encouraging.

"Because these are things I'm proud of," I replied and explained: "The officers were concerned that since people here in Saskatchewan are not as exposed to outsiders as they are in Toronto, they may not be as accepting."

"I see. Well, on that note, you're hired! Those Eastern bastards think we're so ignorant here in the West." With that he stood up and strode out of the room. I was offered a temporary job as the Secretary to the Director of Community Colleges which I graciously accepted.

Much to my surprise, someone from the Ministry of Education during an office tour gave me a warm welcome as the first Pakistani in that office. He directed someone to replace my wobbly chair with a new one; and two days later he even gave me an important assignment in his own office. Those generous advantages made me a ripe victim for office gossip.

I continued to look for other more permanent job opportunities. I applied and got called for an interview with David Williams, the General Manager of a Credit Union. He asked me: "Mrs. Zoberi, did you read our ad properly? Did you see that I require a minimum eight years of banking experience?"

"But that was the *only* requirement I didn't meet," I nervously offered.

"So then tell me, what requirements you *did* meet?"

"Presentable, professional, ambitious, willing to learn… and so on," I replied.

He smiled and promised to call me later. It was the standard brush off. I called him every two weeks. "Mr. Williams, if any opportunity comes up, please call me." But I didn't hear back from him. Three months later, when I least expected to hear from him, he called to see if I was still interested.

I found out that the perfect candidate they had hired, suddenly left due to a problem with the staff. Instead of advertising and interviewing all over again, David thought of calling the persistent lady for a second interview.

"Mrs. Zoberi, my staff hasn't been exposed to people from your ethnic background. I on the other hand have lived in Vancouver, so it doesn't matter to me; but as the only coloured person in the entire place, how would you deal with discrimination if it should happen?"

"I can only add color and spice to your Credit Union, Mr. Williams."

"Young lady you're hired. You just follow my instructions and if there's any trouble, come straight to me, okay?" His smile was clever and his meaningful gaze invited intelligent interpretation. I knew I had acquired a new mentor.

My husband's contract expired so we had to return to our home base in Toronto. This time I found a golden opportunity to join a major chartered bank as an officer in training.

19 years later:

One special day, the vice president of the bank visited our branch.

"We are here to celebrate this branch's outstanding success." After providing us with some sales statistics he announced: "One staff member however, has outperformed everyone across Canada. So… here is the key to…" he put his hand in his pocket as we waited in suspense: "… this is the key to your new sports car… Mrs. Zoberi." It was my name! I was actually rewarded with a GM sports car—a red convertible.

Many of my bosses inspired and guided me as great mentors, regardless of their ethnicity or faith. Canada is a great country where multi-cultural communities can thrive and enjoy their rights. Being a part of this colourful mosaic gives me great pleasure.

(An excerpt from my memoir The Other I *due for publication in 2016)*

Zohra Zoberi *is the recipient of the Literary Arts and Performing Arts Awards from the Mississauga Arts Council. Her poetry, plays and short stories are published in numerous anthologies in Canada and USA. She has published two books:* True Colours *(a collection of prose poems) and* Questionably Ever After. *She hopes to publish her memoir* The Other I *in 2016. She is the Artistic Director of Bridging the Gap (Enlightenment through Entertainment). She received an Ambassador of Peace award from the Universal Peace Federation.*

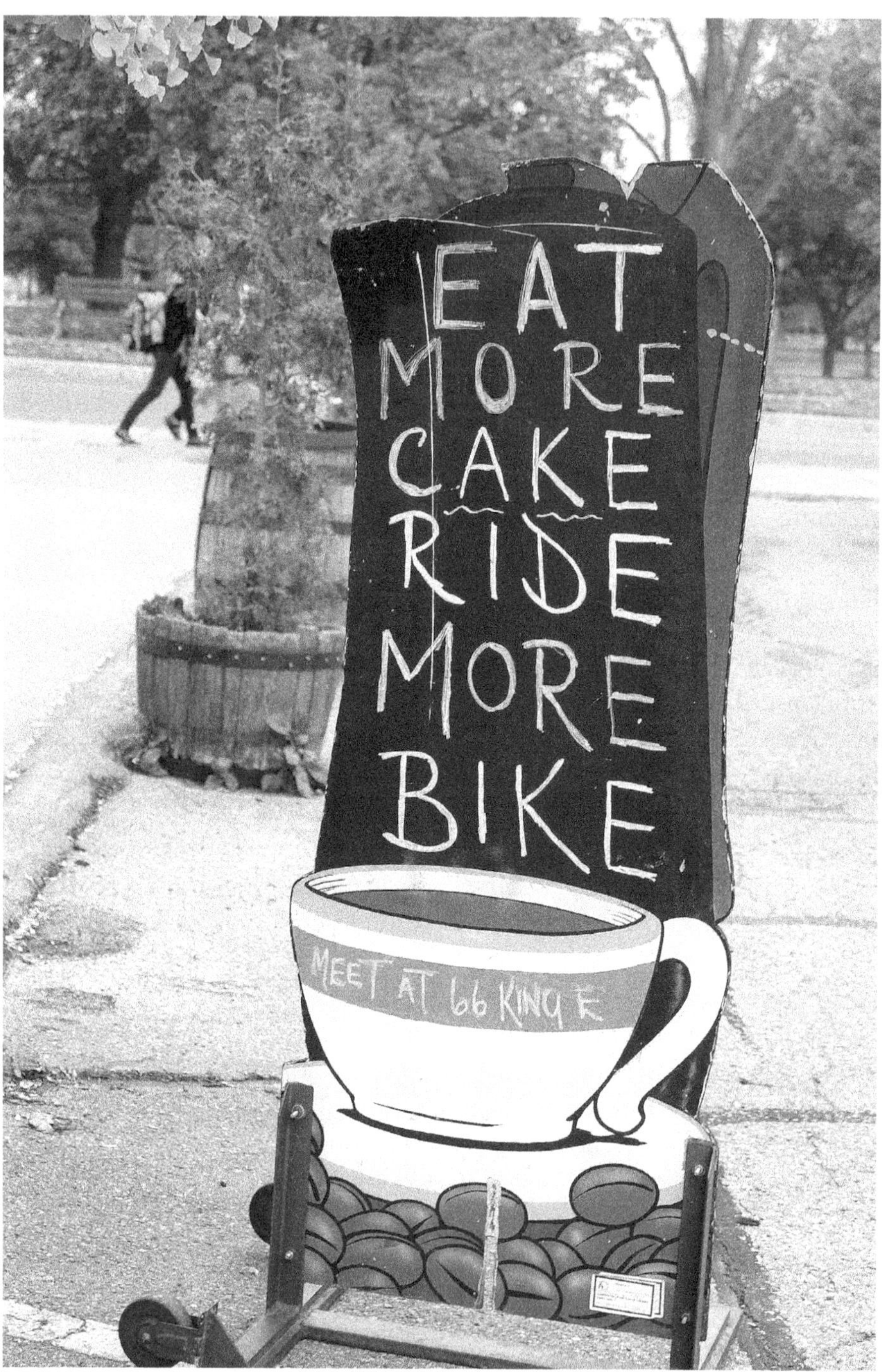

Photograph by Merridy Cox-Bradley

Cheryl Antao-Xavier

I LOVE CANADA, BECAUSE…

Write a poem, children
begin with "*I love Canada, because…*"

Bright-eyes blink
little heads lock conspiratorially
little scribes dig lead into paper
swish erasers, whisk off first thoughts

Would you like to read your poem?
Eager hands shoot up

Hockey and maple syrup
the Ex and Wonderland
spelt every which way
on every list
pizza and burgers, tacos and sushi

pure gems of connection as in
fishing with *grandpere*
amma's roti
Nonna's cannoli

Free verse took flight
finding and losing rhyme

tender beginnings of
"I love Canada, because..."

A COMMON REFRAIN

Gradually, inevitably
old ingrained notions of
'us' and 'them' slough off
dead scales of prejudice
on all sides
growing new skin
from generation to generation

social fabric unravels
is rewoven with fingers of benevolence
and forbearance
stretching across high stakes of Patriotism
standing tall United
under common values Canadian values
engrained in a Charter
aged well over Time

a Oneness that is more of the heart
than of borders and race
that is cleansed, Smudged of
divisiveness
a Creed that soars to
reach heights of Spirit

traditions celebrated
honoured and upheld—Lest We Forget
why we are
and why we came.

Turn then faces
bright with Pride
reflecting the glow
of the red-and-white
Raise then voices
to pledge a common refrain
O Canada…
we stand
on guard
for Thee!

FREEDOM, HALLELUIAH!

thirtysomething
three decades since the
long haul across the globe
flinging Convention to the winds
and the Inhibitions of Culture
Grabbing Life by the short haul
small steps, tentatively, exultingly
relishing the sweet, fresh breath
of Space and Freedom and Spirit

fortysomething
fiftysomething
Spirit continues to soar
to boundless heights
defining oneself by Oneself
comfortable in Skin
and Character and Mind
the Right to Be, imbibed and epitomised
a Voice unrestrained, fearless
a Spirit exultant
gives Praise
Halleluiah!

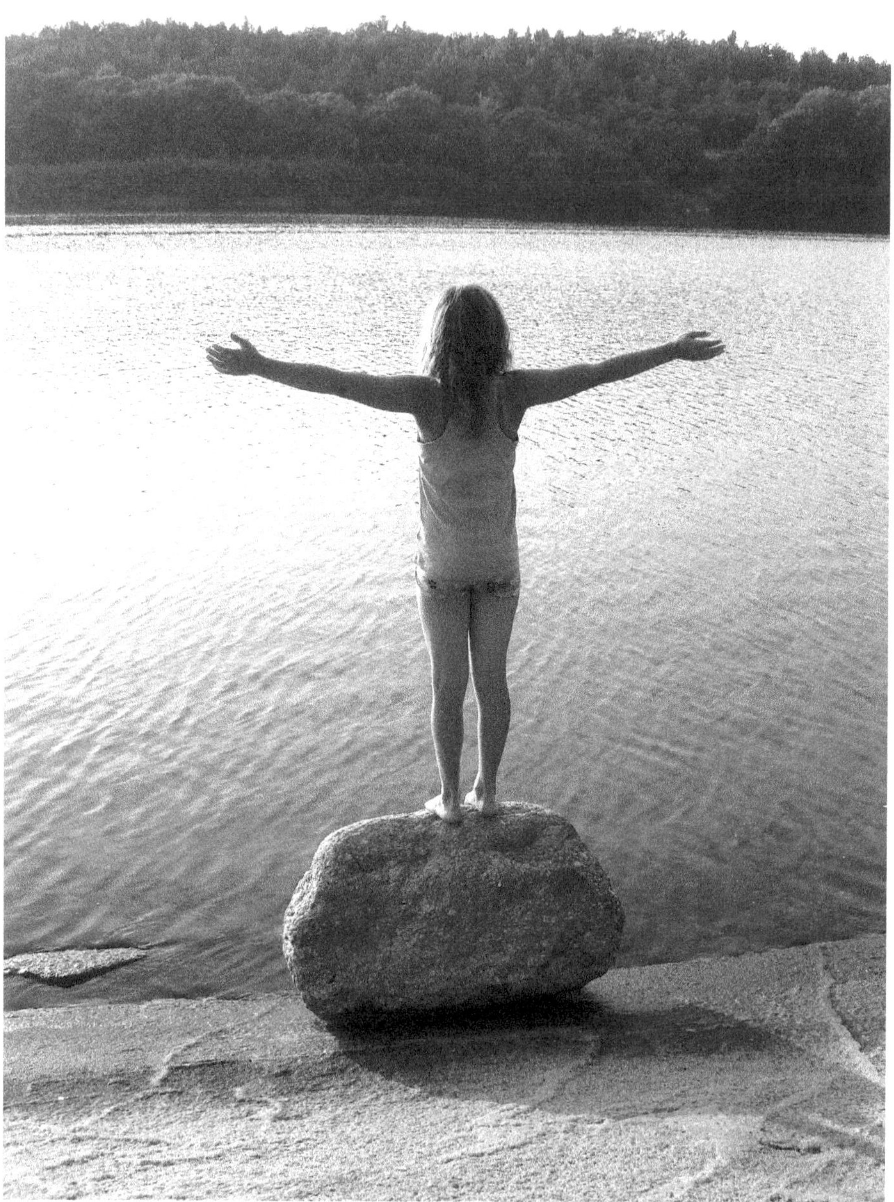

Josephine on the rock by Janine Georgiou-Zeck

HERE, IN THIS LAND

Wordless screams
resonate in the Silence
like dust motes
suspended in sunbeams
There but Not There
seen only when the Light
shines through the Darkness

in this Land—in this Place of Hope
there is Shelter from the Darkness
for those who Dare
push back the bolts of Silence
walk through to the Light
Redefine Kismet
Here, in this Land
—in this Place of Hope.

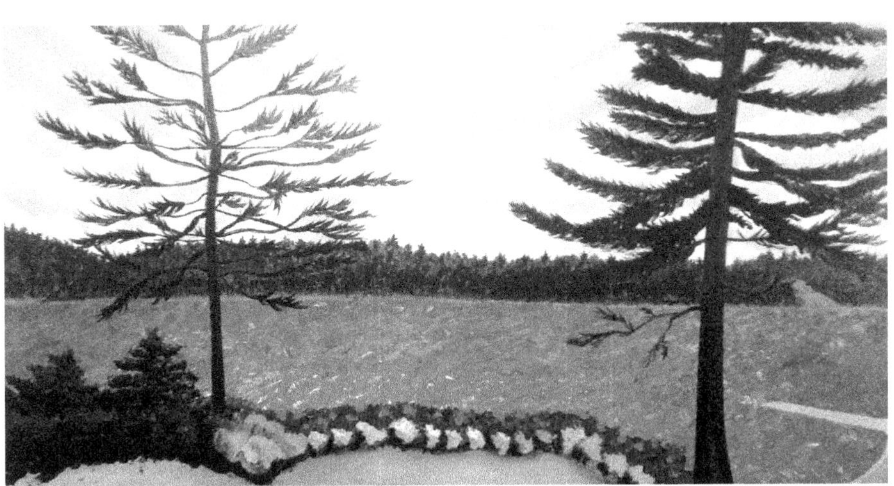

Illustration by Janine Georgiou-Zeck

THE HOMETOWN HEROES

Save your tears for those
Who tie yellow ribbons to trees
Who tuck baby booties in soldiers' duffels
Who slip photos into wallets
Who watch alone baby's first steps
Who explain the absences with fake smiles
Who play roles of both parents
Who sleep alone at night.

Shed your tears for those
Who make overseas calls with anticipation
Who take base calls with dread
Who accept the flag with trembling incomprehension
Who pick up the shards of shattered goals
And piece lives back together
Who honour the missing place
At the dinner table
And on family occasions
Lament their loss of a life for life

Save your tears for them
Our hometown heroes
Who have a share
In that ultimate sacrifice.

UNDER THE MAPLE TREE

Nature creates a little magic
In every single leaf
A microcosmic wonder
To adorn trees in great diversity
In Fall they drop in glory
To scatter and come together
In multi-coloured magnificence
Under the maple tree.

Cheryl Antao-Xavier *is a writer, editor and publisher. She published two collections of poetry,* Dance of the Peacock, *IOWI, 2008, and* Bruised but Unbroken, *IOWI, 2012 and a children's book* Welcome to Maple Woods, *IOWI, 2014. She is working on her third collection of poems and creative nonfiction.*

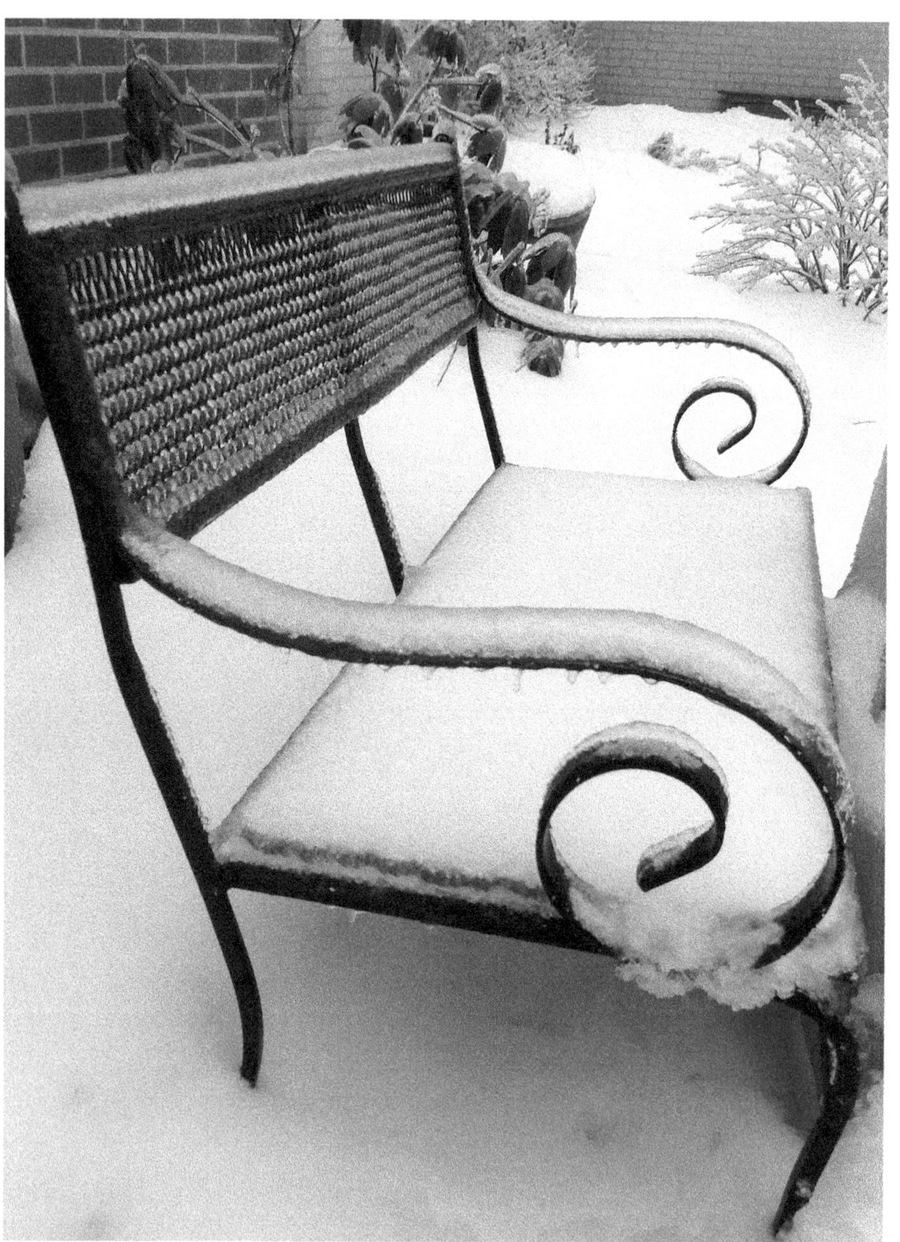

Photograph by Janine Georgiou-Zeck

Jeffrey William Zeck

WHAT IS CANADIAN?

Is it in the LAND?

Mountains and prairies span the globe,
Majestic rivers into lakes run fast and slow,
Rock cut by ice, and water give shape,
To paths traveled through time, early and late.

Forests, fields, flora and fauna of all kinds
Change colours and foreshadow, giving us signs,
Of a cold winter or warm summer,
The cool of fall or spring birds aflutter.

From the longhorn sheep dotting a mountainside,
To the beaver that builds lakes, dams streams so wide,
Whitetail deer that graze and leap through field,
Moose that roam the woods that majestically yield.

The Northern Lynx, a ghost,
Calls of geese travelling to a southern host,
Chatter of chipmunks, defending their hoards,
The knock of a woodpecker, hammer to board.

The call of a raven, and swoop of its wings,
The gobble of turkey in echo rings,
The thumping of grouse, calling a mate,
The piping of ducks in agitated state.

A silent glide by a great grey owl,
The call of a timber wolf, as it begins to howl,
The skulk of a red fox, just before dusk,
A garter snake, releasing pungent musk.

Bears that prowl and roam an area wide,
Loons across lakes seem to glide,
Trout and salmon plentiful upstream,
Dragonflies flit as if a dream.

Corn and wheat fields in wide expanse,
The blowing wind makes them dance,
Cattle grazing in fields of tall grass,
Yet Canada's wilderness will ever last.

Canada's land is ours to protect,
An obligation we pledge never to forget.

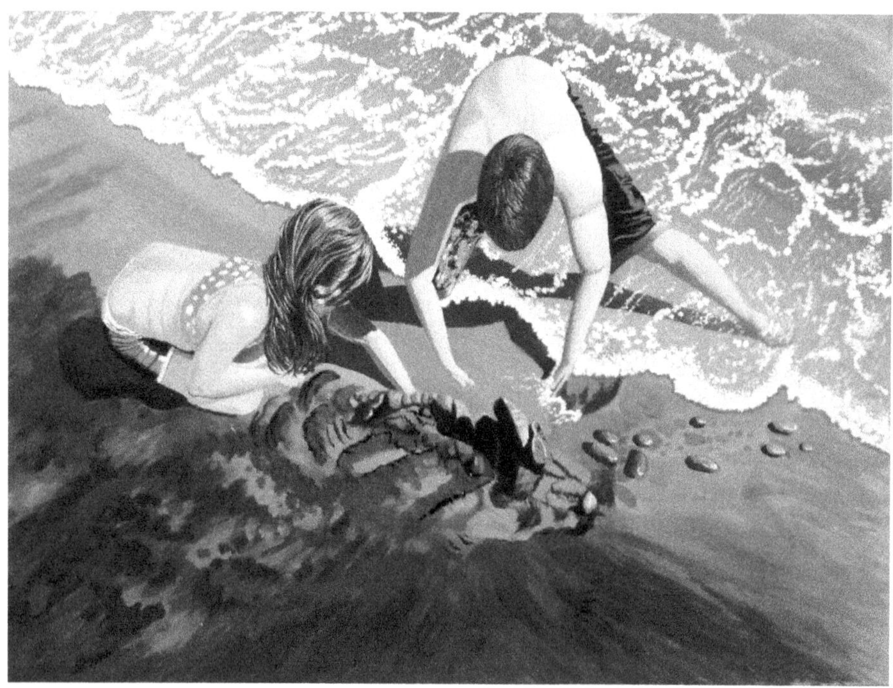

Josephine and Jacob on the beach by Janine Georgiou-Zeck

Is it in HISTORY?

People born as if from the land,
Taking only a need, and not a demand,
Respecting the gift, given by spirits,
Listening to the wild, and able to hear it.

Thankful for life, and paying homage,
Far from what you'd call a savage,
Culture rich, passed down through time,
In stories told and repeated, line by line.

Voyagers in search of this world's gems,
Spoke of peace, and were welcomed as friends,
Soon fell to coveting more in a land of plenty,
Bounty still exists, even to this century.

A British Monarchy expanded its' scope,
Preservation of the past had little hope,
Battles raged on its rocks and in forest,
Throughout time would set its course.

A rich trade of wood, fur, and ore,
Attracted the world that wanted more,
Early settlers of English and French,
The modern world set to entrench.

With it came the new religion priests,
Spreading words of love and peace,
A turbulent time of an early foundation,
To what we now call 'our great nation.'

Canada is harsh upon its' people,
Makes you feel weak, worn and feeble,
But endurance is what made Canada strong,
And Canadians will always persevere on.

Brave to be the first from the foxhole,
Willing to push on when others would hold,
Makes a nation of warriors, who still want peace,
And the sounds of war to forever cease.

Canada's history should be told,
Remembered by us, by young and old.

Is it in the PEOPLE?

People came from cultures of all kind,
A new start and new life, they wanted to find,
They brought a piece of the world in themselves,
That added to Canada such great wealth.

From ancient times to modern day,
This great nation always found a way,
To accept the good and reject the bad,
And do better with what we know and had.

Not boastful but proud of being here,
To be who we are without any fear,
Accepting of differences within our community,
Without hate, judgement, or even self-pity.

Sometimes it is hard, we forget ourselves,
That inner greed, hate, and selfishness yells,
We then come back and realize our error,
Not hate but compassion, to be a bearer.

Polite and mindful of each person's struggle,
No matter how momentous or even if subtle,
Most times we are able to listen and hear,
And treat anyone as our equal, friend, and peer.

It comes from this land and the people within,
Who treat each other well, as if they were kin,
It's a great nation that feels like a family,
We fight sometimes, but make up happily.

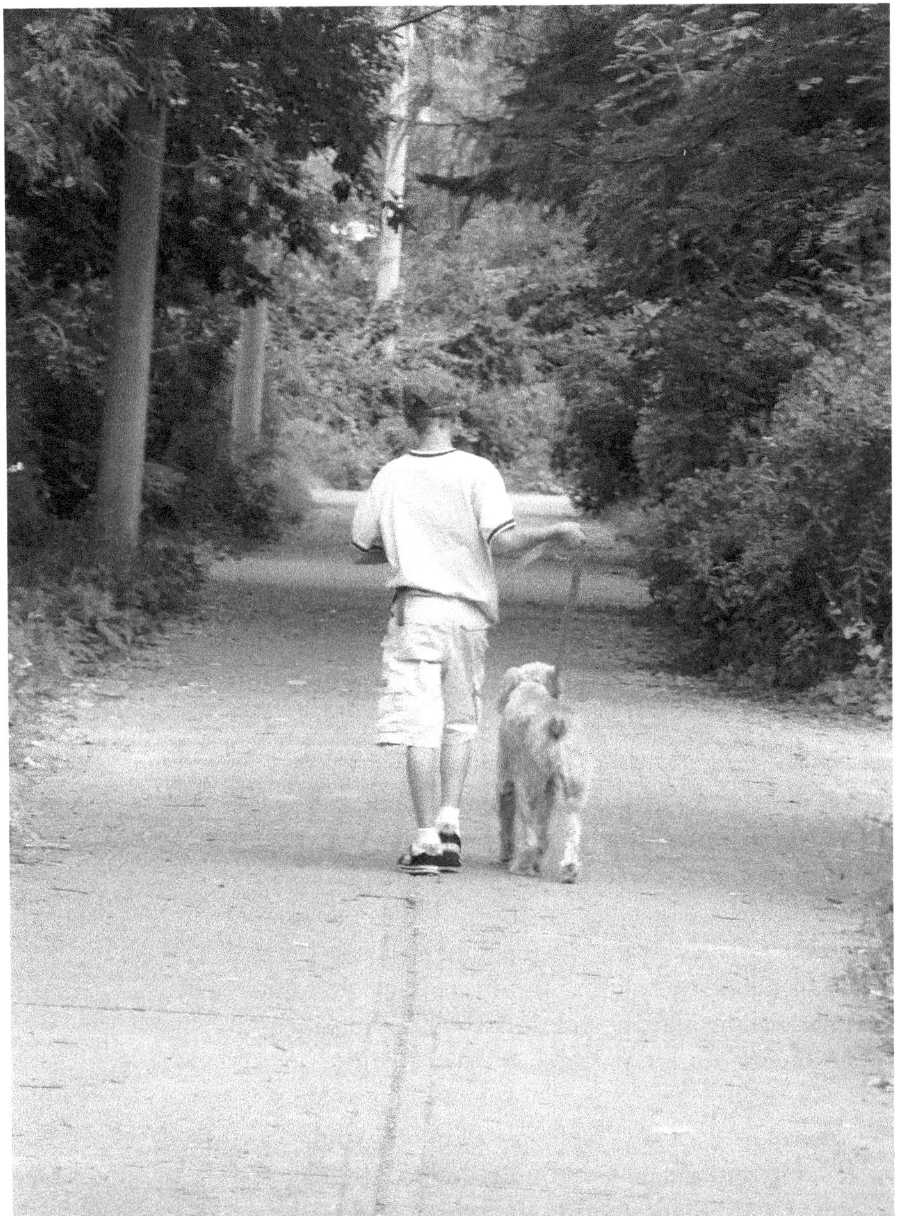

Jacob walking Cocoa the dog by Janine Georgiou-Zeck

We work hard and strive to do much more,
We see it as a challenge, and never a chore,
It's about a nation so big, and people so few,
Always willing to try something bold or new.

When we stumble and fail, we do not stay down,
In defeat and self-pity, we will not drown,
It's about getting back up, after defeat,
Not willing to yield, or even retreat.

Canada's people, should all be proud
Able to say it, and say it out loud.

Is it in SOCIETY?

Our culture is like no other place,
Built from almost every race,
Wanting to protect against persecution,
Freedom of speech and religion is our institution.

A place in the world that others cannot fathom,
Or understand how we make sense of the random,
We thrive in the differences around all of us,
Faith that our people will resolve and trust.

To melt people down in a melding pot,
To blend all the colours, our diversity would rot,
Like soaking a book, and the words run together,
Losing the stories, the tales, we say NEVER.

We live in cities that represent all humankind,
It sometimes gets us in trouble, and in a bind,
There is a clash of culture, and school of thought,
It will never be utopia, but that doesn't mean we stop.

The struggle to include and encompass everyone,
Doesn't always happen, it's not always done,
It's about the attempt at making it work,
To include the differences, wherever they lurk.

It's an amazing feeling, as it all comes together,
It feels like the world has just become better,
To see at the core how people are all the same,
No matter what race, religion, colour or name.

It's about accepting the difference in each soul,
Able to live beside, not above or below,
Equality and diversity, together may seem strange,
It is something we are not willing to change.

We hold strong to a nation with so many,
Cultures, beliefs and ideas, there are plenty,
It is what makes us try to include it all,
Because when it works, everyone stands tall.

'Canadian' is in the land, and in the history,
It's in the people, and part of our society

Canada – so hard to describe, is simply alive,
We look forward to the day, when you arrive.

***Jeff Zeck** is a professional hunt instructor in York Region with over 30 years of hunting experience. He has a genuine love for Canada's natural lands, supporting the care and protection of wildlife in Ontario through his OFAH membership. Jeff is a proud father of three and works for Bell Canada.*

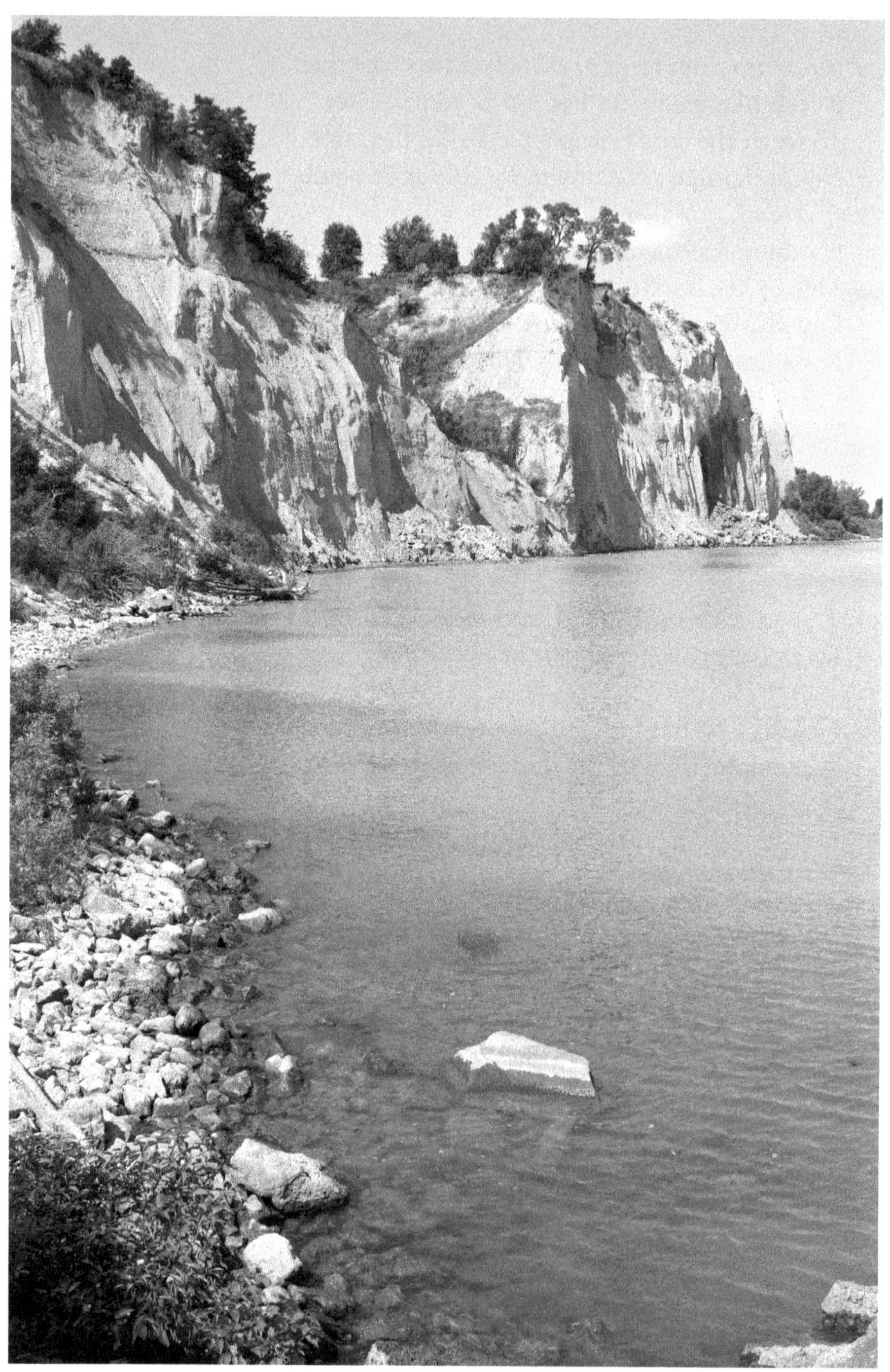

Scarborough Bluffs by Nina Munteanu

Bradley McIlwain

PASSOVER

What happens when we die?

I was thinking
of your funeral
when a hearse

drove by. I heard
a knock in the sky.

The woodchuck
seemed to reply:
I am with you

blowing kisses
on the wind.
Listen for my song

my touch.
I am the warmth
on your skin

when you need the sun.
Remember me
playful

as the rustling leaves.
On the mountain top
think of me

and keep your spirits up.

DISAPPEARED

Out in the country
no one comments
on the tragedy

of an empty picture frame
discarded
in a riddled

farmhouse
only the nostalgic beauty
of its crumbling walls

alone on a hilltop
overcome by the emptiness
of dead evergreens

or the lone cardinal
perched in a broken
window

on winter mornings
mourning the passage
of time

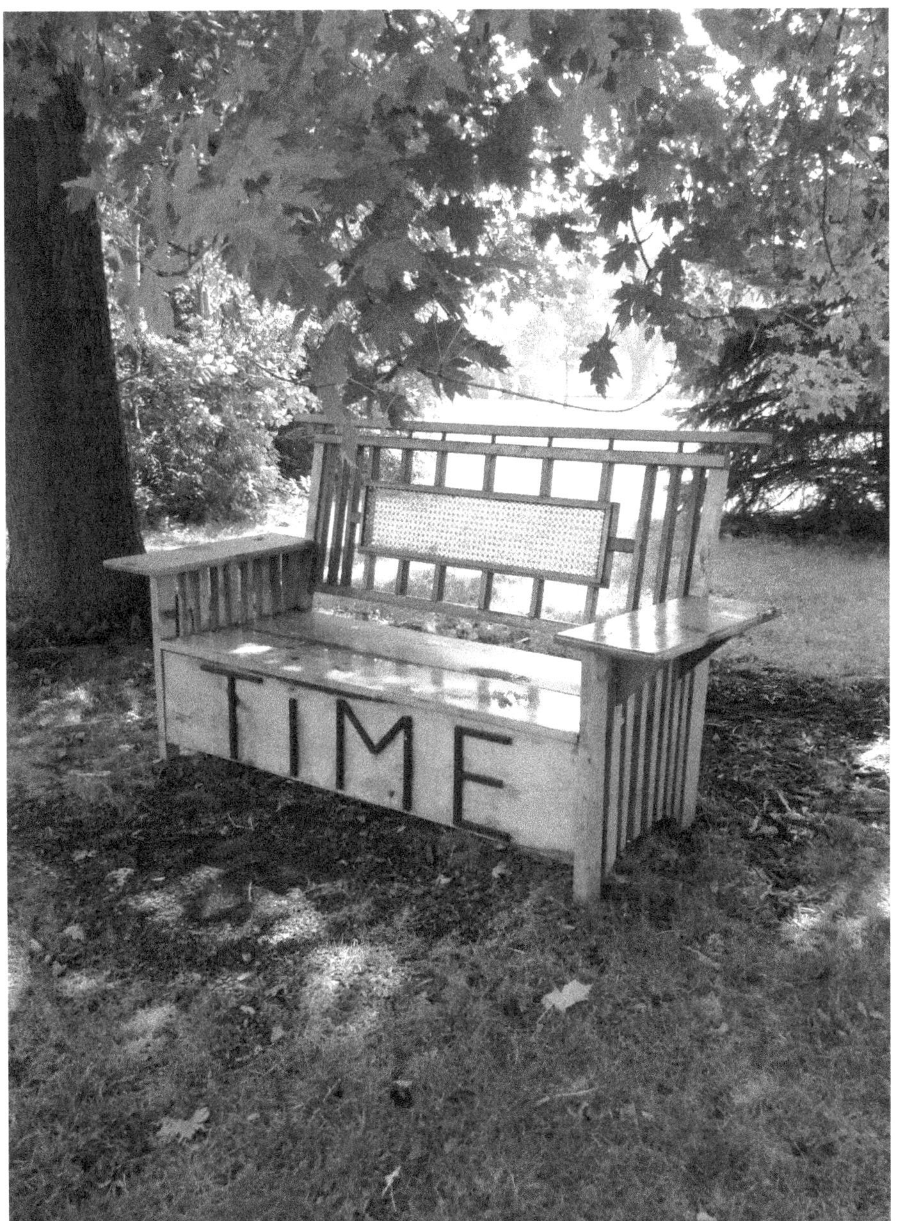

Photograph by Janine Georgiou-Zeck

CHANGE

Penny in a puddle.
Heads or tails?
Centaurs have both.

I *wish* I had more luck.
I *wish* I never grow up.

Change is in the air.
Change for a coffee.

Heads: the face of a
friend I am missing.

She says I drink
too much coffee.
I laugh: both are good medicine.

Her smile is a poem
that affects *change*.

After it rained
I followed the rainbow
to a café on Front St.

you waited
your warmth more
precious than gold

***Bradley McIlwain** lives in Brooklin, Ontario, where he is inspired by the songs in nature, and examining our relationships within it. His poetry has appeared in anthologies such as* Love Notes: A Collection of Romantic Poetry *(Vagabondage Press, 2012),* The 5-2 Crime Poetry Weekly Vol. 2 *(2013), and* Something's Brewing *(Kind of a Hurricane Press, 2014). Bradley is the author of* Fracture and Visiting Hours *(Blurb 2010 and 2012). His third poetry chapbook is* Philosopher's Walk *(Origami Poems Project, 2014). Bradley graduated from the University of Toronto's iSchool, where he received his M.I. in Library and Information Science.*

Milena Marques-Zachariah

STILL GOAN STRONG

Everyone knows we Goans[1] are merry
But when it comes to our daily fish curry
We are serious about how it must taste
Don't believe me? Ask any Tom, Dick or Jerry.

And there is much that I can tell
About our *vindalho* and *sorpotel*
It's hot, it's spicy, it's Goa's own
Though honestly, Mangys[2] cook it just as well.

And then there's that fish lovers' delight
Fish *reichado*, oh what a sight
Whole fish stuffed to the gills and bone
Masala in your mouth at every bite.

Let's not forget the bad word 'curry'
Not for those who cook in a hurry
Devilish little meatballs spicy and soft
Nothing really bad, so please don't worry

We've got to talk about our *ambot tik*
As Goan curries go it's my personal pick
Shark and mackeral, squid, king fish or kite
It's harder on the butt than a donkey's kick

Our chutney sandwiches for picnics are a must
Green coriander, chillies, coconut and just
A little sugar to accompany the salt
You may also find a dollop of dust

And there's a dirty little secret I can't hide
For us, vegetables are just on the side
Fish *caldine*, pork and beef roast those are our mains
Mention veggies and our appetites have died!

To revive again at the queen of all sweets
Ah! *Bebinca*, and *dodol,* and *bathica* are just treats
Caramel custard, pancakes and bread pudding too
The taste of Goa's desserts you just can't beat.

In Canada, Australia, almost every other country,
You'll find Goans settled among the gentry
And along with roast turkey and shepherd's pie
You'll be served potato chops and Xacuti.

Goan then, the truth must be told today
We'll never miss our delicacies while we're away
And though we've taken the Goan from Goa
Goan tastes stay Goan, that's all I can say.

---

1 Goa is a state on the western coast of India. Until 1961, Goa was a Portuguese colony. Goans have a unique cultural heritage and cuisine—mostly Indian, but with strong Portuguese and European influences.

2 Mangys refers to Mangaloreans or people of Mangalore, another state to the South of Goa. Goans and Mangaloreans share a similar cuisine and Christian culture.

BESSIE BISCUIT

"Whose birthday is it, today?" asks grandma Elvira, as she peers into the distance, her brow in a little furrow of worry. "Look, isn't that Bessie heading towards our house?" Everyone sitting on the *balcão* (balcony) stops what they're doing to follow grandma's gaze.

"Oh my God," exclaims her daughter-in-law Martha, "It is Manuel's birthday today!"

Manuel, or Uncle Manny as he is called by all in the village, had just left for Toronto, so nobody was celebrating his birthday at the Misquita home. But Bessie was coming over, and that meant a birthday wake-up call! Bessie never visited otherwise. Only at birthdays and anniversaries. And always uninvited. Bessie walked five to ten kilometres on birthdays to personally wish people. Or so she said. At the end of that long walk, there was always tea, a cold drink, Marie biscuits, and if she's lucky, a birthday cake.

Everybody in the village knows Bessie, and Bessie knows everyone in return. Better still, she knows everyone's birthdays. She left her house at 4 pm sharp, smartly dressed, walking under her faded umbrella that was once black, but was now as grey and misshapen as her teeth. The teeth jutted out, as if too eager to get to all the goodies that Bessie went in search of every afternoon. She was rake thin, always wore clogs, a short, tight dress that looked fine on her skinny frame, and earrings and necklace that matched the dress perfectly. Yes, Bessie had style.

"Bessie Biscuit, Bessie Biscuit," shout some village boys cruelly, for whom she was a sitting duck for mindless teasing. But Bessie doesn't flinch once. She walks on, undeterred, towards the Misquita's home, her head held high, her teeth jutting further with determination. She was on schedule. She had several houses to visit today, and no village *goonda* (hooligan) was going to stop her.

"That woman is made of steel," mutters grandma, good-humouredly, as she sits up in her *volter* or easy chair, where she's been rocking herself ever since she woke up from her afternoon siesta.

Bessie strides up the steps and says, "*Boa tarde* Dona Elvira, where is the birthday boy?"

Grandmother informs her that Henry is not at home, that he has left for Canada. "So, what?" says Bessie cheerfully. "We have to celebrate his birthday here."

The maid is instructed to prepare tea, while Bessie converses in impeccable Portuguese and English to Grandma and her daughter-in-law, Martha.

The tea cozy, made lovingly by grandma, is gently lifted and the tea is poured out from a tea pot. Bessie daintily picks a piece of cake from the plate. Everybody knows she will eat everything on that plate, but she never lunges or grabs. She eats what she can, the remaining she carefully folds into a floral hankie and stuffs it in her purse. The Misquita kids start giggling, but stop as soon as grandma gives them a warning look. Now that the plate is empty, Bessie picks up her biscuit-stuffed purse and hastily bids them goodbye. She's hurrying off to her next birthday visit, a few kilometres away.

After Bessie leaves, the neighbour comes over to find out whose birthday Bessie had come to celebrate. And then, as it happens each time after Bessie leaves, the speculation starts on how Bessie remembers everyone's birthday.

"She keeps a little diary, I bet," says Julie the neighbour.

"I think she simply memorizes the dates," opines Santan, the maid.

"Nobody's asked you for your opinion," Grandma admonishes the maid. "She comes from a good, well-off family, maybe she just needs to get out," she continues. Catch Grandma ever permitting a maid to make a comment against Goa's gentry!

Martha laughs, "She's plain greedy, that's what she is. Why would she risk being teased 'Bessie Biscuit, Bessie Biscuit' by all those cruel village boys?"

"She never comes to our house, so we're saved," declares Julie, smugly.

Ironically, Bessie was picky with class distinction even while she shamelessly paraded her greed. She left the poor folks alone. Or maybe she just knew they would not treat her right. The poor have no time for the shenanigans of those better off in life.

A few years later, Uncle Manuel is back in Goa for his birthday. Whenever he comes down from Canada, he seems eager to take on all the old customs. So the family was celebrating his birthday with a *ladainha* – a litany sung in harmony by Goan village folk. He had returned from Toronto with his pretty wife Luiza, who blushed every time she was asked when she was going to get a '*baba*' – the first son that every villager wishes on new brides. The ubiquitous boiled gram with slivers of coconut is served on such occasions. Fruit cake is distributed by older women who cuff the kids behind their ears if they misbehave. They firmly believe that a child is brought up by an entire village. Nobody dares question that custom.

The men are served 'feni' or coconut palm liquor in shot glasses. The glass is filled to the brim. In one neat gulp, the searing liquor warms the throat and loosens the tongue. Everybody was enjoying a slice of village life, as they sat on the chairs and benches on the long verandah. Later, they would go home, lighting their paths with ingeniously made lanterns–a lit candle placed in half an empty coconut shell to protect the flame from the wind. Some lucky ones, with sons or daughters in the Middle East would have flashlights to lead them home.

"Where is Bessie?" asks Mr. Caetano Fernandes.

Everyone stops talking.

"Nobody invited her?" asks Manuel, concerned. He was fond of her, despite her eccentric behaviour.

"Since when has she needed an invitation?" snorts Grandma. Now everybody stopped munching and gulping. Something's not right. Bessie never misses an occasion.

An old toothless lady, sitting in a corner, noisily trying to munch her way into a piece of cake, says quietly, "Do you remember last week, the church bells were ringing to announce someone's death? It was Bessie."

"Our Bessie Biscuit?" asks a teenager, who is promptly knuckled on his head by his mother.

"Yes," replies the old lady. "She choked on a biscuit and died on the spot."

Nobody laughs.

The man whose turn it is to toss the *feni* down his throat, raises the glass and shouts "Long live Bessie Biscuit."

Milena Marques-Zachariah *is from Goa, India. She is proud of her Goan heritage and promotes her culture through her writing and the medium of radio. In 2012, Milena founded Radio Mango – the only radio program in the Konkani language in the northern and western hemispheres. She produces and hosts this program every Saturday for two hours. Her vision is to keep the Konkani culture and language alive for the Konkani speaking diaspora in Canada. She also writes a blog* Ideas Out Of My Mind *giving insights into an immigrant's life. Milena lives in Mississauga and is very active in the Toronto Goan and South Asian communities.*

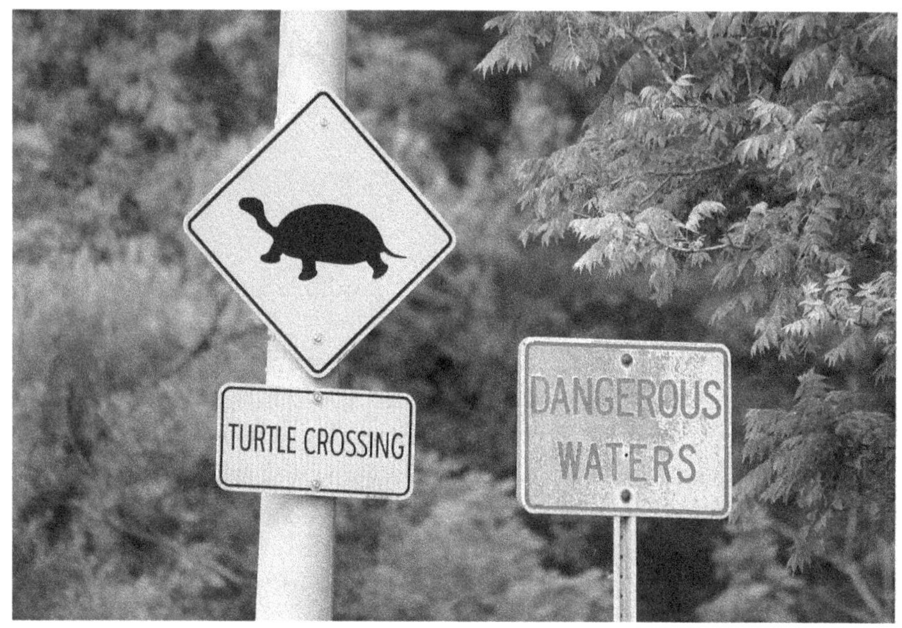

Turtle Crossing Sign by Merridy Cox-Bradley

Viga Boland

THE LADIES OF LORETTO

Grade 9, Day 1, Week 1

I'm scared brainless. Hundreds of girls dressed exactly as I am in dark navy serge uniforms, black stockings, stiff white plastic collars and cuffs and black Oxford shoes. Their Oxfords shine; mine are scuffed. So typically me.

It's September 1960. Like penguins on parade, we are lined up, waiting for the doors to open on the next four years of our lives in the holy halls of Loretto College School for Young Ladies on Brunswick in Toronto.

One small problem: I do not feel like a lady and don't think I want to be one. It sounds boring. I don't belong here. I'm just a girl. But my father, who wants me to become a doctor or scientist believes in attending a school with no distractions from the opposite sex. At fourteen, I'm not distracted by the opposite sex, just attracted to them. However, I know better than to question my parents' decisions, even as I silently resent them for not asking nor caring whether I want to be a doctor or scientist. I just want to be a writer. I like reading people. I hear what they say, but I listen for what they're not saying. I want to write what they don't want us to know.

"Davidah! Davidah!"

Peeping through my unruly hair that never stays where I want it to, I follow the voice directed at one of the most beautiful girls I've ever seen. I stare, awestruck. She's an Audrey Hepburn: superb cheekbones, full lips. All natural. This is before those days of pumped lips, boobs and buttocks. In 1960, what you're born with is what you're stuck with. What I'm stuck with in the looks department is unfair. I glance at the Hepburn lookalike again. She keeps touching her hair. I want to tell her that unlike mine, it's still perfectly in place. I try to twitch my nose like Barbara Eden does in '*I dream of Jeannie,*' mess it up for her a bit, but it doesn't work. No magical powers here, except to perceive that under that aloof exterior, she's probably scared to death too.

She's tall, slim. I'm short, a bit tubby. I hate her already. I hope she's stupid so I can feel better about how I look. I'm ugly, at least that's how I feel about myself, but on the plus side, there's a brain between my ears. When you look like I do, you hope you have something else going for you, or else four years of comparing myself to others in this girls' convent school is going to be slow death.

My girlfriend, Betty, arrives. Betty's a classmate from Grade 8 with whom I have a love-hate friendship. I love her because she's always nice to me but I sort of hate her too because she is so pretty and popular. I asked a boy back in Grade 8 why everyone liked Betty so much. He said, "She has such a great personality." I guess that means my personality stinks because no-one likes me. Maybe that's why I latched onto Betty: I hoped her wonderful personality would magically rub off on me. So far it hasn't.

Betty and I are about the same height but again, she has a tiny waist and all the right proportions. Her uniform fits perfectly around her curves. Mine bunches at my waist, which is too thick, and the hemline is too long. Betty's hemline stops just below her knees, as the nuns' directive dictated. Mine goes all the way down to mid-calf because my father said it doesn't matter as I'm still growing and it will be the perfect length by Grade 11. They bought the uniform two sizes too large so I could wear it for all four years. They did the same with my Oxfords. That's why they're already scuffed: I wear size 7 1/2. They bought me 9's. I will grow into those too apparently. I stick out like a female Charlie Chaplin between all the nicely groomed girls whose uniforms fit properly. It doesn't help to have pretty Betty right beside me but I'm glad she's there. It makes me feel more normal to have at least one friend. What is "normal"?

We're in the classroom now. I sit at the very back. It's a good spot. I can see all of them but they can't see me. That's the way I like it. I slide even lower in my seat hoping the teacher won't see me either. I'd love to be invisible. I daydream about being able to see what everyone else is doing without being seen. What'd be even better is being able to read minds. I'm convinced most people never say what they are really thinking. Of course, odds are we wouldn't want to know either. Knowing what the other girls think of me would probably hurt. But I'd never let them know that. I hide my feelings.

I steal a glance at the teacher. She's a nun, of course… a very old one! She looks like she's been in the convent forever. Her eyes are rheumy behind her heavy spectacles. She removes them constantly to wipe away tears, then slides her glasses back up her nose. Her skin is lumpy. If I didn't know better, she could pass for a witch leaning over a steaming cauldron, and with my luck, I'd be the first naughty child she'd toss in there! But she's not a witch. She kisses the huge cross dangling from her heavy wooden beads and clears her throat. I wonder what kissing the cross does for her. Lo and behold, the witch… er nun… smiles at us.

"I'm Sister St. Simeon, your homeroom teacher," she announces. "We'll now do roll call."

She holds the list of names right up to her nose to read them. She stumbles over each name, even the easy ones. Heaven help me when she gets to my name: it's one of those difficult Polish names that only Polacks can pronounce and everyone else butchers. Here it comes.

"Jad…wee…gah Koob…a…la"

The girls giggle. I cringe and slink even lower in the seat.

"Not here," I mumble. The girls titter and giggle some more. They heard me. Sister St. Simeon didn't. She looks confused. Where did that voice come from? She starts to embarrass me further by stumbling over my name again.

"Jad…wee…ga? Are you… Are you present?"

"Not really," I reply, thinking I'm being funny and smirking a little at Betty who's sitting across from me. She reprimands me with her look, indicating I should sit up and stop being a smart-alec.

I don't know where this cheekiness is coming from. It's not like me at all. Yes it is. I like unsettling people. I don't want to be what everyone expects. That's boring. My father would clobber me if he saw my behavior when he's not around. But he's not here now. That knowledge empowers me. I sit up straight and put up my hand.

"Here!" I reply. I'm cheeky but not mean. Sister's suffered enough. She peers over the top of her spectacles to get a better look at me. I suspect she doesn't think any more of my looks than I do of hers. We're kindred spirits, different only in age. I decide I like her.

The Wallflower

Mercutio:
Nay, gentle Romeo, we must have you dance.
Romeo:
Not I, believe me.
You have dancing shoes
With nimble soles;
I have a soul of lead
So stakes me to the ground I cannot move. "

(From Romeo and Juliet, *William Shakespeare)*

The Grade 11's are studying *Romeo and Juliet* and I'm looking at one of the passages from the play. It sounds so much more interesting than the *Julius Caesar* we Grade 10's are reading. As I think about Romeo's lines, I can so relate when he says he has a soul of lead that so stakes him to the ground he cannot move. He's smitten by Juliet and can't have her. I'm smitten with Dr. Kildare and can't have him, or Ben Casey, or anyone like the handsome actors in our favourite TV shows. My father won't let me date or even go to the CYO dances. I'm really bummed.

"Why don't you come with me one night? It's fun," Betty asks.

"My dad won't let me," I reply and cannot explain any further.

"But why? You're 16! They're all really nice kids from good Catholic homes. I don't get it."

I do, but I can't tell her. That's another secret. But I'm trying to find a way around it. My father likes Betty. I wonder what he'd say if she asked him for me. She does.

"Well, I don't really like Heidi going to dances. It takes away from her studies," my father replies.

His answer doesn't gel with Betty. She might be afraid of mice but unlike me, she's not afraid of my father:

"Oh phooey! We're in the same classes and get the same amount of homework. I have plenty of time to do it on the weekend. Friday night is for relaxing, having fun. Please let her come with me. My dad will take us there and pick us up."

My dad's mouth twitches but he doesn't like losing face, especially to a pretty 16-year-old.

"Okay, just this once," he agrees.

I'm overjoyed. I cannot believe he's going to let me go. Betty and I hug each other and jump around excitedly in front of him. He dismisses us with a wave of his hand telling my mom what silly schoolgirls we are. Mom reminds him we're just normal 16-year-olds and it's time for me to get out a bit.

After school on Friday, I spend hours going through my closet and drawers looking for something nice to wear. Everything I put on looks horrible, stupid! I'm so frustrated. I settle on a form-fitting dark blue winter skirt that comes down to mid-calf. It has a little bow at the back where there's a small split to allow me to walk. It's the trendiest skirt I have and all the girls on American Bandstand are wearing them. Mom bought it for me with the few dollars she had tucked away for herself.

When Betty arrives to pick me up, I want to die. She's wearing a beautiful powder blue dress with a big crinoline underneath, the other most popular style on Bandstand. It fits snugly on her petite waist before fanning out. Her hair is teased. She looks like Sandra Dee in *Gidget*. My hair is teased too but I look like Sam Jaffe on Ben Casey.

"What a small waist you have Betty," says my father with admiration. He looks at me and laughs. "You need to eat fewer cream buns," he continues, pointing to my tummy protruding in the slightly tight skirt.

"And you need to stop buying them," my mother snaps back at him. "Heidi and Betty have different builds, that's all. Now let them go. Betty's father is waiting in the car."

I'm so nervous when we arrive at the church hall. The lighting is dim. I'm almost grateful for that. I'm not sure I want any of these guys seeing how ugly I am next to Betty. As my eyes adjust, I see lots of boys lined up on one side of the hall and we girls are lined up on the opposite side. The music starts but no-one dances. The girls are hugga-mugga discussing which guys are cute and who they hope will ask them to dance. The boys seem to be doing the same. Many of them are looking towards Betty. I'm standing near her, hoping one of them might be looking at me too. But without my glasses, I can't really see who's looking at whom.

As it turns out, I don't have to worry. No-one asks me to dance all evening. Betty is asked time and again. Some of the girls already have boyfriends in the group so they get to dance too. I stand there becoming more and more despondent. This isn't like American Bandstand at all where even the plain girls dance.

"Hey Heidi! Are you going to stand there all evening?"

It's Theresa, another one of my Polish friends from grade school days. We're in different classes at Loretto. She's much prettier than I am... most of the girls are... but she's super friendly. She has been dancing with her boyfriend but he had to leave.

"Well, what choice do I have," I respond. I'm ready to go home. "Who am I supposed to dance with when no-one asks me?"

"Dance with me!" Theresa says cheerfully. "Julian had to leave and I won't dance with any boy but him. But I can dance with a girl. Come on."

Theresa grabs my hand and drags me protesting onto the dance floor. I feel totally ridiculous dancing with a girl, but when 'The Peppermint Twist' comes on, I figure *'what the hell'* and start to twist all out.

Through a blurry haze, I see both girls and guys twisting around the room, but in my immediate vicinity, a handful have stopped and are clapping to the music as Theresa and I give it all we've got. I'm enjoying the attention. I'm good at twisting and I know it. I add some up and down to the round and round when suddenly I hear and feel RIP! The zipper in my skirt splits and my skirt is sliding down. At the same time, the open seam at the back pops the bow and starts coming apart. I'm mortified. I run from the room to the girls' washroom, with both Theresa and Betty crashing through the door behind me.

"Oh my God," cries Theresa looking at the back of my skirt. "What are you going to do? Betty, do you have a safety pin?"

Betty nods "no" but says she'll go back out and ask around. She comes back with two pins a few minutes later and my two friends do what they can to make the skirt wearable. But it's too late for me. The night has been spoiled. I sit on a bench in a far corner of the room watching everyone else dancing and wishing Betty's father would arrive to take us home.

"You're really good at the twist," says a boy's voice beside me. "Why did you dash off like that? I wanted to ask you for a dance."

I look at him in shock. A guy wanted to ask me to dance? As my eyes start to focus on him, I can see why he would ask me: he has a nice smile but big red pimples on his forehead and cheeks. Guess he's a wallflower too.

"So do you want to dance?" He persists.

"I can't. My skirt might fall down."

Perplexed, he looks at me then starts to wander off saying,

"Well there's an excuse no-one's given me before!"

American Bandstand and the Twist

"Have you seen it, Clodagh?"

"I don't watch American Bandstand that much," Clodagh replies, smiling.

Clodagh is the girl with the black curly hair who blocked my view of the honor roll. She has dark, almost black eyes to match her hair. She's very intense, intelligent, and wants to be a writer too. She's a bit like me in another way as well: she's a loner. No-one knows much about her. That's probably why I was drawn to her that day we looked at the honor roll. She's secretive, and I'm curious because I have secrets too. She and I have taken to each other but we only see each other at lunchtime. When we get a chance to chat, it's usually about something deep. But today I'm not in the mood for deep. I watched the happy teens dancing 'The Twist' on American Bandstand the day before. It was shocking, but exciting. I want to know what Clodagh thinks of 'The Twist.'

"So what's it like?" Clodagh asks.

We are in the room just off the lunchtime hall where there's an old piano. Girls are forever banging out 'Chopsticks' and 'Heart and Soul' on it. Clodagh has been trying to teach me 'Chopsticks' but I'm all thumbs. I start to explain 'The Twist' but realize it's inexplicable. I decide to show her instead.

"Hmmm...I need music," I moan. "Well never mind. I'll try to sing it." I start: *"Come on baby, let's do the twist. Come on baby, let's do the twist. Take me by my little hand, and it goes like this: round and round..."*

As I sing, I twist my body round and round, up and down. I swivel my hips, gyrate this way and that. My plastic collar digs into my neck, and my cuffs slide down. I gather momentum, completely lost in 'twisting,' envisioning myself on American Bandstand, with Chubby Checker's voice in my ears. I don't even notice Clodagh trying to send me a warning message until it's too late and a loud voice kills the music in my head.

"Just what do you think you are doing, miss? Stop that immediately!" demands the nun monitoring the lunchrooms. "What is that disgusting display you're putting on?"

Nostrils flaring, Sister's eyes are popping out of her head. I feel my face flushing in embarrassment, but I want to laugh. The shock on Sister's face looks so funny. She asks me again:

"I'm waiting for an answer. Just what was that, young lady?"

"The Twist," I reply, my voice barely audible.

"The what? Speak up so I can hear you."

"The Twist. It's a new ... um... dance."

"A new dance, is it? It looked more like you were having convulsions. Whatever it was, do not ever let me see you doing anything like that again. It was disgusting and most inappropriate to a lady of Loretto. Do you understand?"

"Yes, Sister, I understand."

The nun glides away and as my nerves subside, I begin laughing hysterically. Clodagh flashes me a warning look.

"Shhh... she will hear you and think you're laughing at her."

"I am," I whisper hastily to Clodagh. "I was picturing her trying to do the Twist in those many skirts they wear. Can you just imagine how that would look?"

"Heidi, you're dreadful," Clodagh laughs, "but yes, that would be quite the sight, wouldn't it?"

As we make our way back to our classrooms, I wonder if the nuns ever have fun. Do they listen to music other than hymns? Do they ever dance, skip, play sports? Do they even watch TV?

One thing is certain: I might become a lady of Loretto, but I'll never be a nun.

"The Twist" is too much fun.

[Excerpts from Ladies of Loretto *by Viga Boland, 2015.]*

Viga Boland *is the author of* No Tears for my Father, *2013, which earned her a gold medal in 2014. She followed that memoir with a second book* Learning to Love Myself *in 2014.* Voice from an Urn *is her fourth memoir. Due to failing eyesight and other health issues, Viga expects* The Ladies of Loretto, *2015, to be her last book. This book chronicles her high school days at Loretto College School Brunswick, Toronto. Viga facilitates memoir writing workshops for the Hamilton Public Library, publishes* Memoirabilia, *an online magazine for memoir writers, and most recently, was awarded "diamond" (2nd) author in the Hamilton Spectator's Readers Choice Awards for 2015. www.vigaboland.com.*

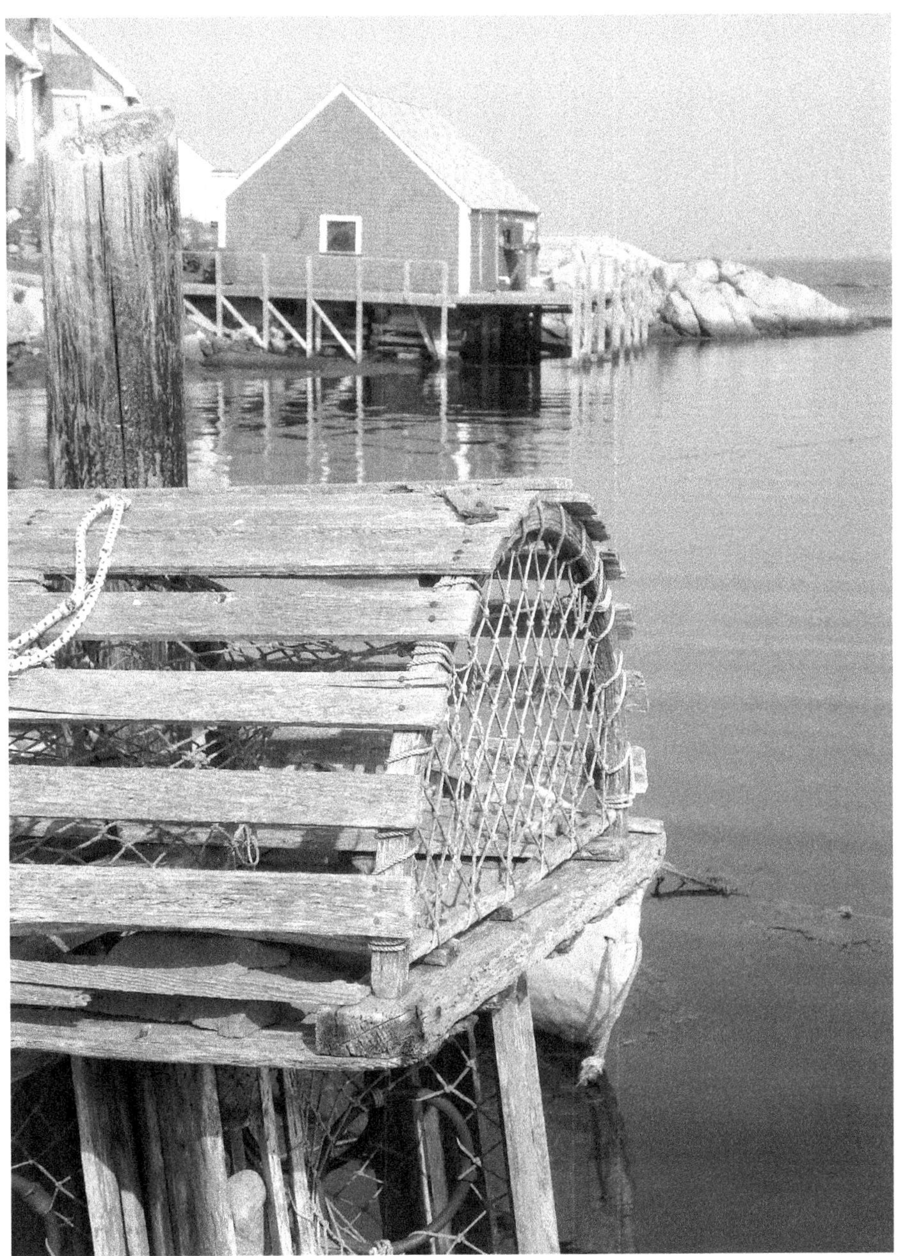

Peggy's Cove by Nina Munteanu

www.ingramcontent.com/pod-product-compliance
Ingram Content Group UK Ltd.
Pitfield, Milton Keynes, MK11 3LW, UK
UKHW020143250726
13967UKWH00002B/831

9 781926 926582